Selected Poems 1967-2014

Also by Trevor Joyce

Sole Glum Trek
Watches
Pentahedron
The Poems of Sweeny Peregrine: A Working of the Corrupt Irish Text
stone floods
Syzygy
Hellbox
Without Asylum
with the first dream of fire they hunt the cold
Take Over
Undone, Say
What's in Store: Poems, 2000–2007
Courts of Air and Earth
The Immediate Future
Rome's Wreck

Trevor Joyce

Selected Poems

1967-2014

Shearsman Books

First published in the United Kingdom in 2014 by
Shearsman Books
50 Westons Hill Drive
Emersons Green
BRISTOL
BS16 7DF

Shearsman Books Ltd Registered Office
30–31 St. James Place, Mangotsfield, Bristol BS16 9JB
(this address not for correspondence)

www.shearsman.com

ISBN 978-1-84861-352-2

ACKNOWLEDGEMENTS
The poems in this volume are drawn from the following publications, with
permission of the publishers:

with the first dream of fire they hunt the cold. A Body of Work 66-00
(Exeter & Dublin: Shearsman Books &
New Writers' Press, 2001; 2nd ed. 2003);

What's in Store: Poems, 2000–2007
(Toronto, ON & Dublin: The Gig & New Writers' Press, 2007);

Courts of Air and Earth
(Exeter & Dublin: Shearsman Books & New Writers' Press, 2008);

Rome's Wreck (Los Angeles, CA: Cusp Books, 2014).

Dates following poems indicate first publication.
Notes to some of the poems are available online at
http://www.shearsman.com/

Contents

For Anna

Capital Accounts

(Worked from the Chinese of Lu Zhaolin [635-84])

Through this long peace
arterial routes
intersect
with narrow lanes.

Beasts of burden,
black and white
drag coaches
of sweet-smelling wood,

and jade-inlaid
sedan chairs
cross recross
the town.

Past celebrity glitz,
old money dens,
golden accessories
circulate.

Dragons gnaw
rich canopies
glinting
in the early sun;

phoenix vomits
glittering lace
under crimson
evening clouds.

One stretch
of gossamer
encompasses
the trees;

assemblies
of magnificent birds
unify the groves
with song.

•

Birdsong
unifies the groves,
moths flicker
through the thousand gates.

There are emerald trees,
silver terraces,
colours
you don't have names for.

Forked galleries
with window bays
assume the form
of leaves,

and ridge tiles
linking towers
are phoenix wings
at rest.

The Corporation's
ornamented halls
rival
the sky,

and the Executive's
immortal works
overreach
the clouds.

In front
of the high-rises

not a single face
you know.

Imagine!
On the streets
you encounter
only strangers.

•

What about her,
who puts on airs
facing
the purple mist?

In the past
she danced,
oh
how she danced!

It's like she's blind now
in one eye;
would another
cure her mind of death?

It's like she's lost
one of her arms;
and she's sick of dying
bit by bit.

•

She's sick
of the sight
of the hale
and hearty,

those eternal soul-mates,
joined at the lip

never tired
displaying themselves.

It's depressing
to see
a single phoenix
in brocade,

but a pair of lovebirds
glued to the screen
will cheer you up
in no time!

•

The paired lovebirds
glide and flit
around the decorated
beams,

through the turquoise
hangings,
fumes
of turmeric.

Fashionably permed
and teased,
her hair
is cutting-edge.

Eyebrows
pencilled crescents,
next she applies
her war-paint.

•

War-painted
and powdered up,

she exits
to the chase.

Quite
independent
yet appealingly
vulnerable,

she changes
expression more
than is strictly
necessary.

Boys ride by
on thoroughbreds
as dark as
iron cash.

Hookers do trade;
hair in the dragon style,
with bent-knee
golden pins.

•

At City Hall already
birds
are coming home
to roost;

in the gate
of the Supreme Court
sparrows
brawl.

High and mighty
vermilion walls
overlook
the boulevards of jade;

the azure cars
slip down
beyond the golden
barricades.

Joy-riders
on the look-out
roam
the blank estates,

while hit-men
make
their contracts
in full light

and fat cats
in hand-
tooled footware
deal strict cash,

till all are drawn
down the same side-street
to the hookers'
sweet emporium.

•

The hookers
in the darkening
put on
flash stuff,

and then with purest voices
sing
familiar
sentimental airs;

in the outskirts
night on night

figures visit
like the moon,

at the heart
each morning
traffic gathers
like clouds.

•

Both the outskirts
and the city's heart
are conveniently situated
just off the freeway,

while major transportation routes
provide immediate access
to the financial
district.

Supple willows
and green ash
bend
touching the earth,

through sultry air
the red dust
joins
the sinking sky.

•

Now you arrive,
you civil guards
of this our state,
a thousand strong,

to drink
green wine

from nacre
cups.

Gauze boleros,
jewelled zones
are stripped
for you,

for you,
dance turns exotic,
and the throat
grows deep.

•

Then there are the big men
go by the name of
"Minister"
or "General":

the sun and sky
revolve
around them
and they yield to none.

Presuming respect,
these proud spirits
suffer
no reproach,

such high grasping
can't endure
nor recognize
restraint.

•

These great men
unrestrained:

their vehicle
the storm.

They claim
their music
and their sports will last
a thousand years,

offering
their power
and wealth
for our example.

•

In the cycle
of the seasons
change comes
instantaneous,

or
chard
ocean
switch,

gold steps
and white jade halls
become
green pine.

•

Silent
in the emptiness
he dwells,
attentive.

Nothing
is happening

but flowers
on the mountain:

falling always
falling through
his reach
they fall.

(For Patrick Galvin, 2003)

earlier
even than
morning

yet the
hands
are hard
at work

the maid
yawns in the
straightened
room

factotum
promenades

gun
cools
dust
settles

while the goods
are fenced

loan sharks
with lone
wolves
coevolve

world-up!

(*For Owen*, 2007)

Tohu-bohu

I   First things first. One time a friend of mine came in for a few empty crates from a Mazda import agency. With a couple of rolls of felt he transformed his poky yard into a well-appointed loft where he kept fantails first and pouters, then tumblers, and finally some serious racing birds. At that juncture the fancy breeds had to go because their freaks disturbed the steady fliers. But he never banded his soft birds for racing, or bothered with the mandatory clock, just released them when he rose and let them settle back at evening to roost reassuringly secure. In the end though he got thoroughly sick of their ceaseless moaning, so he kicked out the lot of them, refitted the wire grilles with glass, sanded, sealed, and papered down the primitive walls, screeded the floor, and later on moved in himself, the family, and all their traps. For a good week after in these novel quarters he picked over an odd volume of Pliny's *Natural History*, shaken intermittently by the indignant refugees beating like stormy rain against the panes, and on the flat felt roof. This is a true story.

II   *...do not look upon me on the dung-heap*
      nor go and leave me cast out
      and you will find me in the kingdoms.
  And do not look upon me when I am cast out among those who
      are disgraced and in the least places,
      nor laugh at me.
  And do not cast me out among those who are slain in violence.
  But I, I am compassionate and I am cruel.
    Thunder Perfect Mind

When the shattering
key turns clockwise
the golden tumblers fall

through courts
where suits
are duly packed and paid

the ward turns
from the crooked talon
lofty strut and pinion

down their powers
and dominations
to the striking jack

III   And now these carriers
wheel painfully aloft
ringed round with tokens

protocols addresses
codes conventions empty forms
and the streams freeze in their shadow

remorselessly they brood
on every post
spill milk

and thick saltpetre
as they flap
from the twisted pair

to coax
all the news
comes down

so tell me
how would you put down
a lingering infestation

of goddamned angels?
set snares of blood
raise ghosts

and memories
for decoys
bait deadfalls

with true sleep?
or keep by the fire
a niptic cat

to stalk high winds
and pounce
on fallen stars?

they just don't get
the message yet!
suggestions please

so I can get
forever shut
of their close breath

fat with clay
stone floods
the midnight crashing

of their verminous wings

(For Clare and Tom, 1995)

from The Poems of Sweeny, Peregrine

It was the end of the harvest-time precisely. The cry of the hunt and the bellow of the running stag carried through the wood; Sweeny suppressed his initial fright and chanted of the trees of Ireland, and of his grief.

This done, he took off once more across the summits of the land, and each leap was mimicked by the hag until at last he sprang from the battlements of Dun Sobairce and she faltered in pursuit; she fell upon the sea-cliffs and the rock broke her. A catspaw played with her wreck.

Fearful then of Loingseachan's vengeance, he wandered on, coming at last to the land of the Britons. He held the castle of the king of that land upon his right side and came upon a forest, wherein he heard sounds of lamentation and anguish. Sweeny entered the forest and found there another madman, the Man of the Wood. Each recited the aetiology of his derangement, and the two entered upon a contract of friendship: "Sweeny," said the other, "we have exchanged confidences, now each must be the other's guard; he who attends the crane's call break above the blue and turquoise waters, who hears the lucid cry of cormorants, the clatter of a woodcock's wings, snapping of spent wood, or sees birds' shadows on the roofing boughs, let him give warning; two tree-trunks shall divide us and if either hears any of these things or similar, then let us flee, swiftly."

For a year they were together; then the Man of the Wood had, perforce, to go to where his death awaited him, to be snatched by a gust into a waterfall to drown. He delayed only until Sweeny had told him his own tale just as it is set down hereinafter, then sought out that fatal and elementary conjunction, and the fall included him.

Sweeny went back to Glen Bolcain. There a madwoman pursued him until Sweeny divined her madness and turned, whereupon she fled before him. This he made the subject of his chant, strophe and shrill counterstrophe.

He did not stand. His course brought him back to the home of his old wife Eorann, where again he came to grief; she, seeing his wretchedness, rejected him. On Benn Boirche, a peak among the southern ranges, he found such rest as he could take, victim of storm and graupel, and retold the shifting numbers of his ways.

XII

Life is loud in the glen.

Frail stag,
          your cry has halted me;
now I am sick with sudden longing:

odour of herds from pasturelands,
stag bold in crag and sky.

Oak, broad and leafy spire;
good fruit bends the hazel wands.

Gap stopped with dappled boughs,
bright alder boughs;
there are no blood specks on my skin
as I move on.

Blackthorn: barbed wine. And this
above the pool and on the pool, sparse
and sour green,
          cress.

Saxifrage and oyster-grass
are a green path. and see
this ochre, fallen fruit,
this apple-tree.

Mountain blossom. Mountain ash.
My flesh has dropped in a crimson net;
briar, drunk-thorn briar.

Yew is the little churchyard tree,
and where the night of wood congeals
the ensnarled darkness is named 'ivy'.

In hollyboughs I hide from storms,
I hide from the clubbed ash too.

Verge of a dark wood,
vertical chalked motif,
slender, silver, coiling, lovely
birch.

Aspen is swift; its leaves
sing like a distant war;
green blade smashes green blade.
Then, for a time,
                    silence.

In forest glades
my dread:
oakwood pendulous in wind.

XIII

Mountains are rivered slopes,
brown rock and scree;
I would sleep if I were let
in green twilight of Glen Bolcain.

Water; light through green glass,
wind bright as glancing steel,
the ouzel sips the vivid spring,
cress green as the ocean's ice.

Slopes littered with tough ivy,
thin willows blade the mirrored streams,
yews are intense and many there,
birch is the dim glen's lamp.

No act could hold me, Loingseachan;
I would break frosted routes up Boirche.

You were a scabbard of iron words:
father and mother
daughter and son
and brother dead;

supple sweet body,
bright wife
gone to earth.

I am a cave of pain.

XIV

Dense wood is my security,
the ivy has no edge.

Though the lark pursues me,
summed, I take the dove

that crosses, and am no red hawk.
Shadow of the rising woodcock,
blackbird's scream, disturb me.

I stoop to see the little fox
a-worrying of the butchered bones;
he has more shifts to seize me than the wolf.
The guileful fox, the murderous wolf I shun,
scumber and filth befoul them.

Light folds and bends in the chill ice
of pools, and I am cold.
Still, the heron is at sedge,
the badgers squeal in Benna Broc.

Here there are ample stags
to turn much fallow with the share,
but no hand holds
the stag of high Sliabh Eibhlinne,
the stag of sharp Sliabh Fuaid,
the stags of Ealla and of Orrery,
the fierce stag of Loch Lein,
the stag of twin-spurred Baireann;
each stands at rest on salient ground.

Sweeny, I, swift visitant of glens;
rather, call me Man Run Through.
O stag, I could lie down
among your jagged tines
in pointed luxury;
now I await the final point.

See the royal stag go by
dressed in his tattered velvet.

Ronan Finn compelled me here.

XV

My sleep is sad
without feather-bed, numb
from the sharp air
and the grit of the wind-blown snow.

Cold wind with ice,
ghost of an old sun,
shelter of a single tree
on this barren table-land.

Striding through rainstorms,
pacing the mountain deer-paths
and paths through grass
in the orange frost at dawn;
stags are belling
in forest copses,
the paths of the deer are sheer and hard:

I hear the hammer of the distant surf.

O great God above
my weakness is also great
and black are the sorrows of Sweeny
whose scrotum hangs slack.

XVI

Four winds fetch many miles
to meet in me, am as a fifth,
fluent and cold. Boirche
is perilous: so deep
its silent reaches, power
of secret currents threatens me.

I have not yet forgotten
harvest-time in Ulster
around quivering Lough Cuan;

I have lived in Ossory
and within the glades of Meath,
now their springs inhabit me;
in the aftermath of fruit
observe such exaltation:

I sift the debris of the shattered woods.

(1976)

Joinery

through no imperial portals but rusty bars on broken hinges
    iron epochs spans past understanding

        fold back on themselves doubling their ghosts twice dying
    past locks rain seized while the sleepers dreamt

        and bore into the catchment wearing further down
    across the long constructed courses indeliberate lives

    the vegetative agents work their slow approach
        ages remembered in the ratchet of a thorn

        now against gravity they lift and hold rest and again advance
to this kingdom of black earth like dampened dust

where my green knight evades the black shawled witch's eye
    the covert grows encompassing

        retainers dreaming round their table of contents
too much attached can forfeit grip

        water spills from the cup
    again flame starts from the fire

    from what was lost never delivered
        when this spell of silence ends

        in rage abandon grief and love resumed
the dragon's teeth and the sly pervasive worm

bells beyond the kingdom toll the significant hour
    abridging others which therefore augment

        their weakness with a going back a gathering whose returns
    diminish with their distance from that source

yet they engross and are not waste
these ages picking over the midden of words

the news results and forecast take their toll
effective against accident elsewhere not here

through which all paths are critical
and the streets are silent the squares empty

in his gaslit room of the golden birds
soft shadow and the glinting song compel

attention and all utterly absorbed
that flight of colour from the hard matter

lifts to compose itself in such startling light
whistling unconstrained by bars

property removed from ground and here
selects this its imponderable element

nested within boundaries of breath
roosting quiet as the small rain of summer

the old man receives the boy's green gift
the secret bears itself and dies

and neighbourhood of speech transforms
as late return from something long since lost

the beam strikes root the shaft grows ripe
low ceiling vaults to sky

he reaches through the element of birds
against the gravity the golden drift of dust

breathes past all passage in this present now
and the green knight hears his golden song in wonder

(*With & for Michael Smith*, 2000)

COUMEENOLE

Dig! you cried

We dug out great trenches
and extended the abyss
down into an utter darkness
that stopped the heart with its cold

We fought off monstrous beasts
that nudged and butted us with their blunt heads
and from those regions of terror we brought back
massive rocks and curious shells

We threw up huge walls
and ramparts to repel
the encroaching forces
of chaos and disorder

We took all the boulders and all the sand
in the world and ranged up
mountains into the clouds
against the combing winds and the hard sea

And in the territories we had created
we established order
we set up high towers riveted with light
and we built roads castles and cities

At evening as we left
looked back and saw whole continents dissolve
under the flood and heard
the soft collapse of walls and boundaries

you cried

(*For Owen*, 1995)

SEVEN SONGS FROM
TURKIC & FINNO-UGRIC

The truth
I dreamed
I craved
sweet fruit.

    At the heart
    of the mountain
    seams of silver
    shine.

    Eat up, drink up,
    enjoy yourselves,
    while yet our shining
    world survives.

Like last year's
winter wheat my hair
scarcely sprouted
and was shorn.

Like green timber
my soft bones
scarcely sprouted
and were shorn.

    I set down oats
    behind the barn,
    now comes
    the scythe.

    Ah, my cousins,
    my dear friends,
    now comes
    goodbye.

At break of day
the nightingale,
I thought my mother
called me home.

In the white night
the cuckoo sounds,
I thought my father
called me in.

    Green the sleigh,
    and blue the harness,
    good colours
    for a white-faced horse.

    Behind your back
    I speak your faults
    however you
    protest.

In the dark wood
swifts don't fly.
What's a blue dove
doing there?

With no mother,
with no father,
for you, what lies
in store?

(*For Marja Gaynor*, 2007)

Syzygy

The Drift

and then there is this sound
that starts with a scarcely audible
rustling inside gold the whisper
echoing within the diamond
grows to take in snatches
from high stars from elsewhere
the disintegrating actions
of clocks so that eventually
you attend to the infinities
of numbers shattering
the shriek that is the change
of several millions

•

the red fish leaping from the mouth
up the cold fresh stream
to the empty source
spilling down
through stars and through
the watching courses of stone
until the fixed mesh abstracts
unerringly each hour
with all its clamouring brood
jerking routinely to the tune

•

noise of concerns sequestered
ultimately will get out
states sundered bleed
surely each to each
by breaking bounds ghosts
traffic through the empty squares
stay mum and the child will answer

even what it must not know
which you realize cannot
but end in an exposure

•

bones may well
bring meat to market
on the road voice lodges
in the fine apparatus
of the throat
there to recount
the exaltation of the source
disclose the system
shock of close attention
and to the distracted hearing
it sounds a history
of all the ordinary
aches we suffer

•

when the thieving
that was well advanced faltered
the imperial presence surveyed
the ordered territories
and declared in measured words
nothing there is savage any more
intelligence and griefs are tamed
rage is reduced in parks
only perhaps along the furthest bounds
may be some dirt a little ghost
and these are even as we speak contained
in three quart jugs

•

sea will fit full of fish of many orders
these will be my varied meat
then surface craft with manifests

for relish weed for bread
abyssal waters for cold broth
though scarcely yet begun
finished already
and to follow
garrisons brief zones
of time and influence
the tempting metals of the air
do not they fly and last of all
bright asterisms will fit in

•

in three quarters now you lie
lacking a fourth
of your voice that flew at once away
not a tremor breeds within the marble orchard
and is it that this simply is either finished or not
or not yet begun
perhaps truly not begun
twig of bone empty still
until there come the words
now quite forgotten whats the air
the sun leans down
and lifts the sea

•

jugs standing sealed and safe exhale
intoxicating the rare earths
dark matter in the air
there is nothing either
fishing the empty grounds
the heavy elements
turn over in their sleep
uncertain ever
when the filling
when the thieving

•

millions are too vast
cruelly they hunt the fields
and bring down awkwardly
the quickening in its course
behind their staggering weakness
leaves devastation and impersonal rage
but even these may be attended to
outside the foundries where they sleep howling
as sometimes fierce and weary
one will sprawl and rest
its harsh throat on your arm
and then there is this sound

•

the tune of several mysteries
what brought this on
the sand whispering
in your veins
what wind of knives could
buzz the nodding headbone blind
what soft amends
the clock disintegrates
the sun does not rise
the dream is mistaken
pulse of sand is
roaring obliterates the red

•

exposure to the extreme
stillness of fire
the flickering rock
disturbs
all night across an empty sky
the high frosts creak
and strike the clumsy sun
leaves on the grass
the shadow of the vaulting white

beyond the bounds
no silence no noise

•

we suffer an old vertigo
that strikes with the first dream
of irresistible winds
across these settlements
thats how the unhinged
thrones and dominations fell
attending as joints lost their grip
throughout the deadlocked centuries
as new wood broke
disordered from old stock
voices were joining
in a round of bones

The Net

and then there is this sound the red noise of bones
when the thieving sea will fit in three quart jugs
we suffer an exposure to the tune of several millions

fish that concerns may well bring
full of fishers now you lie that was well standing
the extreme old mysteries are too vast

starts with a leaping meat sequestered
lacking sealed and advanced of many orders these will be
vertigo that strikes stillness cruelly what brought this

ultimately scarcely audible from the mouth up to market
faltered the imperial my varied meat then safe a fourth
on the sand with the first dream of fire they hunt

the cold rustling on the road will get out
surface of your voice exhale presence
the flickering of the fields whispering

inside gold states fresh voice
that flew at once intoxicating craft with surveyed
irresistible winds in your veins rock and bring down awkwardly

lodges in the fine the whisper stream sundered
the ordered away not a tremor manifests the rare
the quickening across these settlements disturbs what wind

bleed echoing apparatus to the empty
for relish weed earths territories breeds
of knives thats how the unhinged in its course all night

source surely each within the diamond of the throat
dark and declared for bread abyssal within the marble
across an empty could buzz thrones behind their staggering

grows to each there to recount spilling down
in measured orchard matter waters for cold
and dominations the nodding weakness leaves sky

the exaltation to take in by breaking through stars and through
broth though scarcely in the air and is it that this simply is words
devastation fell attending headbone the high

bounds the watching snatches of the source
there is nothing either finished or not yet begun
blind frosts as joints and impersonal

courses ghosts disclose from high
there is nothing either finished or not yet begun
creak what soft amends rage but even these lost their

stars from elsewhere the system of stone traffic
perhaps truly savage already and to follow garrisons fishing
grip throughout may be attended to and strike the clock

shock until the fixed the disintegrating through the empty
the empty brief zones any more intelligence and not begun
outside the foundries the clumsy the deadlocked disintegrates

squares mesh of close actions
griefs are grounds the twig of bone of time and
the sun sun where they sleep centuries as new

abstracts attention of clocks so that eventually stay
empty still tamed rage is heavy influence
leaves howling as wood does not rise

you attend and to the distracted mum unerringly
elements turn the tempting until there come reduced
broke sometimes fierce the dream on the grass

hearing each hour and the child to the infinities
metals in parks only perhaps along the words over
and weary the shadow is mistaken disordered

will answer even what it must it sounds of numbers with all its clamouring
now quite forgotten of the air do not the furthest bounds in their
pulse one will sprawl from old stock of the vaulting

brood a history not know which shattering
sleep whats the air may be some dirt they fly and last
white and rest of sand is voices

of all the ordinary you realize the shriek jerking
of all bright a little ghost and these are even uncertain ever when the sun
leans
its harsh roaring were joining beyond the bounds

cannot but end in aches routinely that is the change
down and lifts the asterisms the filling as we speak contained in
obliterates throat on your arm no silence no in a round

we suffer an exposure to the tune of several millions
when the thieving sea will fit in three quart jugs
and then there is this sound the red noise of bones

(1997, 1998)

Construction

A. 1. I had just turned off from Stephen St.
      Into Great Ship St., was confronted
      By a massive grey stone wall.

      The late rain lay in patches
      On the pavements, shone
      Between the grey-green cobbles

      Of the roadway, throwing up
      Grey facets of built stone.

   2. The cobbles were enamel,
      Chipped away in places,
      Showing the basic texture
      Underneath; grey rock.

B. 1. This was suave ceramic
      Fired in the mind's furnace.
      I had to look again.

   2. Each individual limestone cuboid
      Chisel-squared and weathered
      Rough and grimy, holding on its face
      All its past history and the threat
      Of its future. Streams
      Of rust-brown rain had stained
      The entire wall; each
      Block realized its presence
      In this pattern and the wider
      Patterns of sunlight, shadows, tone

      And the complete distributed
      Weight of rock
      Combined for the present.

C. My brain had built
A scheme of echoes,
Of ancient meanings held
In rock, in sunlight on ice,
In the low beginnings of thunder

But this wall needed no exterior
Aid for its stability,
No echo in its circumstance.

(1967)

Diagram + Sun

A thin gravel of coal,
of grain and shattered glass
glistening preciously
in the shadow of a slag-heap,
in the huge darkness of a crane.

that circles the sun
like a searching blade.

Grouping doves
stab after corn here
and the shape of the high gnomon
plays across their plumaged
dove-grey heads and subtle breasts
and gradually the chipped glass
dulls; the prisms sift no more
bright fluids and the waters
slow.

Through hours the river halts,
reverses and the dredgers swivel round,
dragging their stern-ropes out.
the rustle of a tautening hawser
furrows the sapphire dusk.

A lissom fog vaulted the debrised channel
to see its shape scored glaucously.
the tart air moults a sultry ash.

Tight bars of steel
mount like elongated boulders.
a golden bird swoops
to its eyrie
high on the cragged metal.

A sabre crane-boom scabs
the throbbing blue aorta
in a brutal pivot.

Two locked sparrows drop
out of an alley's mouth;
the small grenade squawked,
fractioning,
jolting the feathers down
onto the river's skin
to be sloughed
in another ocean
and another time.

And someone,
              maybe a child,
                        asked;
'aren't birds strange'
                  and
'has the sun bled all away?'

(1967)

they found
a bucket
filled
with tears

now they demand
whose property
is this

who so
decries
their state

no need
they say
not now

so why this
weeping
without owner
function
future
why these tears?

(2006)

cut a god
the wound
destroys
the knife

slaves
are easier

simmered
honey
and red
flower
of copper

smeared
generously
the green
wound

discharge
watery
and thin

she died
in the night

she was
a barbarian

(2005)

successively
each emperor's
doubles were
assassinated

then
himself

therefore
this stratagem

our latest
emperor
was chosen
secretly

no-one
informed
not even
the elect

it worked

somewhere
he lives
obscurely
on

quite
unaware
he is
a god

(2006)

barbarians
are bad
at walls

ours keep
them out

hordes
break
like a river
against
our bastions
and then
flow on

sweet
orchards
gentle
hounds
we have

the hands
of slaves
draw us
sweet
water
up

(2007)

Verses with a Refrain from a Solicitor's Letter

As when a faded lock of woman's hair shall cause a man to cut his throat in a bedroom at five o'clock in the morning; or when Albany resounds with legislation, but a little henpecked judge in a dusty office at Herkimer or Johnstown sadly writes across the page the word 'unconstitutional' – the glory of the Capitol has faded.
Benj. Paul Blood

Dear Sir, I was this morning
straight after the news and forecast
hanging from an old appletree in my garden
a small Japanese bell
when I received through the post your importunate
and quite misguided threats

and in this regard time shall be made of the essence

An injunction, you say. An obstruction,
you say. You've a lot of chat for someone
that's not even clear who he's talking to.
Does this help: not only have I
not erected any obstruction
in the form of a barbed wire fence or otherwise

and in this regard time shall be made of the essence

but I'm attempting today to rest and recover
from the effects of an obstruction in my own passages?
I have, it pains me to have to spit it out, a strangury,
and you've got the wrong man, chief,
I've better blockages to worry about
than the one at the back of some godforsaken hotel in Midleton

and in this regard time shall be made of the essence

What's more, my bell is mute.
The inscribed slip that made its tongue
chime in the wind, flew off. It's not my day.
Far from putting up barbed wire fences,

I'd prefer, right now, to see one of those bright Byzantine
Christs come striding across from the opposite hills

and in this regard time shall be made of the essence

fresh from baptizing Adam, vast and very masterful,
lugging a patriarch along with each arm no doubt
from some new-harrowed hell
and scattering from his feet a fine debris
of locks, bolts, spancels, cuffs, gyves, fetters, stocks,
and other miscellaneous hindrances

and in this regard time shall be made of the essence

And what would our Neighbourhood Watch do then?
Put the polis on his tail, stay home, and watch that hooligan
as he'd come, breaking contracts, flattening fences
and leaving gates and prisons open behind him.
Yes, he's the man would soon break down
the calculus that stopped my flow

and in this regard time shall be made of the essence

And not like a thief in the night,
but openly I'd have him
eliminate all limitations,
peel walls and roofs away like rind
and with his knife of stars
reveal what soft exotic fruit grew ripe within

and in this regard time shall be made of the essence

unchain Prometheus from his rock
to stretch and scratch at last and fire
stones at that bloody bird,
allow Eurydice ascend
to feel the strange dew fall
chill through her faded dress

and in this regard time shall be made of the essence

remove the ratchet from the clock, North
from the needle, run the many down to one. (Oh no,
hold on there, God, we can't have that!
I won't be one with our friend the illicit
erector of barbed wire barricades,
or this damned notary. Cut!)

and in this regard time shall be made of the essence

It's evening now. The bell's transformed.
With a laurel leaf lashed to its tongue
it cries out clear in the wind.
I'll just sit tight till the Ipral sets me up
and I no longer pass blood,
or feel weak when I attempt to stand

and in this regard time shall be made of the essence

take idle note of that shrill song:
past flight and hot pursuit
terror passing cold restraint to come
then when I'm up to it again, forgetfully,
turn that stock still.
I trust this terminates our correspondence, Sir

and in this regard time shall be made of the essence

(*For George Hitching*, 1995)

The Fishers Fished

dark within darkness
let them approach
that dry estuary
whose waterless wave
brings down
the gravel of worlds
to a bed of sand
because the diamond
is feeble and restless

leave them be guided
to the motionless storm
by the evidence of trees
and mineral structures tumbling
slowly through the hushed light
so they may see
this still disturbance
reach deep within the wrenched metals
making them whole

have them discover
flame without fire
where it adjusts itself
brooding on wood and stone
that they may bind
apes and lower vertebrates
and lay them under its blue claws
and after gather them again
unharmed and whimpering

they may set
nets below
the fish leaps
nets above
the fowl flies by
fires within
the flame scorns

withdrawing
through stone
or settling
in the open sky

then they are snared by water
wind devastates their dreams
and fire nests savagely
above the derelict jaw

(2000)

The Course of Nature

If heaven too had passions even heaven would grow old

Li Ho

Poor angels their high regard
fixed beyond the outer
horizon of stars

with tranquil fascination
watch the generation
and destruction of worlds

their urgent stride
shatters the capitals
of empires their serene

breath and thunderous wings
blast continents and seas
until sometimes randomly

distracted by the stray
falling of a small songbird
the delicate drift of white

ash inside a furnace
their eyes clouded
with unbearable pain and weariness

oblivious of their feet
bleeding from flints
vast wings moulting

and raw with neglect
newly they survey
all the tiny and discrete

effects of the world
and weeping to witness
such quick and irreversible decay

they stoop to gather them
into eternity and so
become the prey of immense

cats that sniff them
out to maul and play
fully dismember as they dine

on the rare giblets
of felled seraphs
and their squab

(1995)

from Rome's Wreck

[Translated from the English of Edmund Spenser's Ruines of Rome]

Maireann lorg an phinn, ach ní mhaireann an béal a chan

III

You look for Rome in Rome, do you?
In Rome no Rome is to be found,
these same old walls and gates you see,
such wrenched halls are what Rome men call.
    See then what wreck, what waste is left,
and how that she, which with such strength
tamed all the world, comes weak to heel,
the prey of time, that eats up all.
    Now as the grave of Rome, Rome serves,
as Rome and no one else quenched Rome;
her course that runs fast to its end
still streams on through, still falls: Vain world.
    That which is firm now flits and fails,
    and that which flits is still and stays.

VII

You high sad wrecks and views, you Rome
all fake but for the name, you tombs
that still hold safe the brief slight fame
of souls long gone up to their Gods;
    arch that's pure win, spires shot up so
they scare the sky, tick tick, too bad
that bit by bit you end in ash,
scarce worth a laugh, your spoil our source;
    though for a time your frames make war
on time, yet time in time will wreck
your works and names, and sour your dregs.
My own sad wants, rest at your ease,
    if time make end of things so sure
    it will end too my pain, and you.

IX

Hard stars, and you, you gods as harsh,
skies of sheer spite, you too, false world,
be it by rule or just through chance
you shape the acts on earth of men;
    why, long since, did you work, so hard,
to make this world that lasts so long?
Or why were not these halls of Rome
made of some stuff as strong and hard?
    I don't, as does the mob of fools,
charge these, all things that move through moon's
light, dolls of time that run to dust;
no! I say this (though I don't care
        to cross those minds at odds with me)
        that one day all this all shall cease.

XXXII

And is it that you hope, my words,
that you'll be heard through worlds and times
to come? Do you have hopes verse lasts
while years turn, modes change, and men fail?
    The skies grow dark. No fame stands fast
or these stones spread round, clean cut, cold
and hard, dressed by sharp steel, so far
less frail than script, should have it made.
    I use the tools I've got: hard words
passed down, passed on, may speak on some
days when the live voice breaks.
Not all words bear the weight. I mean;
        but they may not. And these? Pen's mark
        lives on, but not the mouth that sang.

(*For Fergal & Marja Gaynor*, 2009, 2014)

Without Asylum

true we may surmise
how a knife hatched
out of meat
should fledge

span with blade
then unexpectedly
take flight onto some sill
moult there with clutch

of fist falling from it
arm with balance
of muscles altering
to lift and lay

its murderous
intent and disturbed
dreams and brood
how everything broken

so they say points
to the unbroken
forgetful is it of what did
the breaking as I witness

my own loathing
and desire walk
through the dreaming
labyrinth of my child

while detailed depositions state
how further on
within the wood
whose skew bent

registers which wind
prevails itself perpetually
ragged and worn
from ocean breath

and sun and every flame
it quenched in its far
fetch the bright axe
blossom suddenly

the long bones lever
up from it like anthers
and beyond the startling
calyx of teeth

an avid buzzing perishable
fruit set thicken
and disintegrate
to load with sweet

secure deposits
of afflicting gold
their remote cells
and stipulate eventual

shelter from the fall
asylum from the edge
a luminous domain
unbounded

seldom they relate
why the innocent whose mouth
is like a bowl of blood
blurts words already

darkened with gods
and sacrifices how
I have the face of those
whose faces have rotted

and although whirring blades
have been observed
to crystallize spontaneously
throughout the native

rock and ramify
in gangs and casual crews
good companies exfoliate
pervasive and exotic dust

where tellers and their firm
controllers fight to reconcile
accounts and sound
is severed from the dogs throat

there is no further testimony
to the effect how in this
realm of agents deeds
and instruments

one sees at last displayed
an armoured beast whose
head a growth of flame
in the shadow of the ripening

clocks the river sames
destroys itself the jug
absconds leaving to the grasp
only a sustained bewilderment

like dice spinning

(*For Angela*, 1998)

The Turlough

It is raining elsewhere

Vertical rivers reverse
stone floods
the karst domain
each sink turns source

Rock brings forth fruit elsewhere

The action of the clock
runs down
through fissured hours
wells up lost time

All is not lost elsewhere

The emigrant returns
old loves
reach out their arms
gold leaves fly up

Time heals all wounds elsewhere

Bullet returns fire from flesh
to gun
the dried stain weeps
bone knits again

No mark gets the cold deck elsewhere

Boxed by his court of spades
Jack wakes
from his stone watch
that springs each arch

London Bridge is falling down elsewhere

Circuits and gates collapse
in sand
the face the glass
composed breaks down

Raw head finds bloody bones elsewhere

Vast hands stop at the stretch
knuckle
of blazing gas
and wrist of stars

The gods explode this turn elsewhere

Red giant and white dwarf
come in
in a blue shift
Venus meets Mars

There is thunder now elsewhere

Under an incandescent sky
flash floods
spread out this lake
is on no map

(*For Celestine*, 1992)

Lines in Fall

1   Bag of bones cant lie down
     to night
     timbers settling
     crack them up right
     under Orrery Hill

     head waters run bone dry
     springs stop
     fall rains fill up
     resurgent courses
     where the flood divides

     the fabric all washed up
     gives way
     to thread bare ribs
     remnant the wave un
     weaves in ropes of sand

     the loose ends ravel out
     until
     the form breaks down
     its raw material
     and nothing else survives

     this cataract cuts off
     all lines
     into the past
     the old tissue far
     too slight to stand that fall

II   the face turns
     stone ground
     in the fall moon
     cold peregrine in transit
     fret to bits

where a hard
rain picks
this dream to shreds
a sharp wind in the easts grip
combs bones straight

that head long
home ward
warp from the well
dressed frame falls as the sand sifts
down silts up

groundless fears
stop then
now that yarns spun
out the flocks blown far afield
from tenters

bare ruined wires
run way
beyond these lines
night weaves new cloth the moon
her shuttle

(1995)

say

how was
the table
set?

were the
knives
angled
just so?

did one dog
loiter here
another there
multitudes
yon?

what was
the appearance
of the man
in her bed?

i foresee
empires
laid waste

(2007)

some forty
years later

approaching
the capital
they heard it
rattle and
wheeze
like a toy

once within
only with
difficulty
maintained
balance

on streets
still slick
and caked
with human
fat

or was it
twenty?

(2007)

presence
of the angel
of death
is generally
acceptable

even following
a series
of happy
scenes

it adds
a certain
weight

difficult
to achieve
by other
means

having small
children
play naive
divinities
may also
work

(2007)

Tocharian Music

In these mountains there is a stream which flows away drop by drop,
producing a sound as of music; once a year, at a certain date, these sounds
are collected and made into a musical tune.

Wu Kong

Still the jade woman circulates the cup
its empty now

Too long interbred with dragons
they grew restive
and rebelled
against the imperial mandate

Eleven thousand
died in the reprisal
and the city laid waste
the airs dispersed
only the names survive

Time slipped out of their tablature
and without stopping
fled
fugitive amongst those sands

(*For Máire Herbert*, 1995)

The Peacock's Tale

The costume of the people is so wretched that, to a one who has not practiced such visitations, it is almost inconceivable. Shoes or stockings are seldom to be seen on children and often not on grown persons, so yet they stand shod only in the plush of their red bogs, making unsteady verticals.

The rags in which both men and women are clothed are so worn and complicated, that it is hardly possible to imagine to what article of dress they have originally belonged. Duds, threads, fatigues and once-fancy hand-me-downs step out in parallel, all swaddled in knots, bedizened in glad rags; wardrobes run down past the least coherence.

It has been observed that these sheer beasts never dismantle themselves of their clothes when they go to bed; but the fact is, that not only are they in general destitute of blankets, but, if they once took off their clothes, it would be difficult to put them on again. Is not this a terrible way to be naked: wanting spread or comforter, however mute; to lie in envy of the gravel under grass?

Thus, their habit is worn day and night till it literally falls to pieces; and even when first put on, it is usually cast-off fragments; for there is not one subject out of ten who ever gets a coat bespoke, but chaff away instead their little means at hazard, where at last, exposed by numbers and for lack of other stuff, they pawn the nails of their fingers and toes, with shirred and smooth and shaggy, even to their kelder and dimissaries. That's the way they walk in view: tender and fractious, unsheltered and exposed, while yet not wholly detached, as the moth waits famished and the needle rusts.

> God!
> Just think
> of all those pianos
> standing
> with their white
> tusks
>
> splayed
> in anticipation of toccatas.
> So toe

that foxtrot,
    glide
        your finery,

and be glad to be in the first
    frush
        and you'll get by.
Chaffer away
    as the spitfire
        blooms

run
    above you.
        Untache yourself, would you,
and get up
    on that stone
        like a bloody peacock!

Get yourself into
    the swim.
        Sure, any animal
is "disfigured"
    when disrobed of its
        hide,

"and cold too,"
    as the motley
        sow
remarked to her farrow.
    Unbrace yourself there
        in front of

the warmth.
    Let that uniform
        out a loop
and join us in the next
    tranche
        laundered.

The bunny hugs
    its burrow
        as the addict
does his coupon.
    You can never have too much
        exposure.

But I cannot lie!
    Bleach
        leached once
even into my livery,
    quite stemmed
        that old cashflow.

I'd a damned sight sooner
    break
        into a pavan
than go higgling
    with those demons.
        Let the cast of them

go splat
    and which of you would raise
        a finger
to get out?
    Climb past these
        unmentionables let you.

The human
    is a thing
        who
walks
    around
        disintegrating.

(*For Fanny Howe*, 2003)

from Outcry

(Worked from the Chinese of Ruan Ji [210-63])

Blood-sweating
    horses breed
    in the extreme west,
from times past memory
    their drovers
    herd them east.

When spring and fall
    drive hard
    without remission
how then can wealth
    or rank
    resist?

Clear dews glaze
    the orchids
    in the marsh,
white hoar-frosts seize
    the level
    plains.

In the morning
    youth
    is soft,
late at evening
    age
    is hard.

We hold
    in perpetuity
        no grace.

Morning,
 I scale
 the precipice;
evening,
 descry
 remote massifs.

Thorn-brush
 invades
 the plain below,
gregarious
 birds
 flicker up.

In solitude
 the phoenix
 dwells,
discharging
 the inheritance
 of its kind.

Heaven and earth
 are by a single tree
 conjoined;
account
 all other plants
 mere show.

Around,
 through forest
 undergrowth,
the fattening
 bindweed twines
 and thrives.

Seriatim
    phoenix rise,
    flapping vast wings
to test
    the limits
    of cosmography.

Quick tilt
    of pinion:
    see them ride
the jet-stream
    and obliterate
    space.

They break their fast
    on windfalls
    of eternity
and sup
    exalted
    outside time.

Should these
    who haunt the blue
    fear nets?
Should such
    consort
    with primitives,

disclosing
    old
    vacuities,
trading
    coarse
    tags?

As a boy
      I grasped the sword
and easily outfenced
      my masters;

clean strokes
      sliced the clouds
till skill
      bred notoriety:

my sword chopped
      at the desert edge,
my horses drank
      peripheral chaos;

banners whipping
      the wind
joined gong and drum,
      my only music.

War is a sheer affliction,
      furious and sad;
boyhood
      bitter.

Exiting
    by the Eastern Gate
I sighted zones
    beyond the markets

where austerity has secured
    sufficiency,
and nature keeps the kingdom
    peaceable.

I was engendered
    in an evil age.
Frost stiffens now
    my rich brocades.

Foothills
    and summits
shiver in the chill
    air.

Under heavy
    clouds
darkness
    is thickening.

The migrant geese
    long gone
only the raptor
    shrieks.

Mode mood and time
    crash heart
to a white
    void.

(*For Mary FitzGerald*, 2003)

Twin Relative Deposition

2 years of watches remark the end of autumn

Subtle as the leaking stench of gas
that trembles the slight web of sleep
they died; and so quick the dead
lose their composure, moulting age with face.
all habit broken and all gesture discontinued.

The dandelion, frost-quenched, watches in the house,
marks time along the well-path; lion's-tooth
that emptied cheek and jaw of meat,
hiding in the hollow house now, waiting
near the well where the neighbours don't go now.

Soon even the memory will be gone,
the old woman and her brother will be a broken habit;
the neighbours will compose new plots;
the well-path will be overgrown;
well forgotten, covered by a policy of growth.

Lion's-tooth, famished at the acrid lakeside,
re-mounts to the village as the mercury drops:

oil bright in a crock,
    flame tilting at the wick;
        blue-herons in a bladed bay.

        last autumn month.

(1969)

Christchurch. Helix. 9th Month.

Passages of labyrinth repeat;
the crypt gives vellum thighs to the dead,
mark our return in this way;
again we hollow dust-caves, ankle-deep.

Paths are furrowed by rats' feet,
scribbled as cryptic schemes, motifs
of death and propagation;
here the fruit of death dilates.

Arid courses interplay, rivers of dust,
graphs wrought in frost, dust-falls interpret sunlight.
A cat plays knucklebones with something grey
and we move into daylight:

for mornings the roads are chrome
and the sun is a citron stain on a limed wall.

(1969)

Mirror: Of Glazier Velázquez

Where shutter, wall, and lock
exclude the casual sun
a new light illuminates
long darkened and abandoned rooms.

Light that is natural has failed;
an angular course delivers this
through systems of reflections,
enfilading in its route
chambers where pose manifold
still dwarf and her princess
introvolute and incessantly,
or where, upon a bed, a graceful girl
approves herself in slender contemplation.

For such enlightened scenes we shun
the menstruant whose searching gaze
strips of the mirror its validity
(so brilliant Paracelsus says);
its silver and austere control being lost,
the glass once more perspicuous,
carved wood frames only chaos,
and all slenderness and grace are gone.

Since obex, jamb and baffle block
all natural constellation
we had no thought to see things clear
in our enforced obscurity;
but this enlightenment gives shock
as to see small private things
of our familiar lives, estranged in the inverted vision
of the encrypted dead.

Now in a bright spontaneous chute
the light rushes on the glass
as did that old and Jovial gold assault
attendant Danaë for her engendering

an apotropaic and more polished
hero for epagomenal days.

Enfiladed are the dwarves
that with painter, infants, kings and queens
fill out an ordered zone
in the impulse of the gold
to reach that buried silvering.

Expectant of such crescent light the dead
wait in their vaults as did that Danaë
horizontal for the God,
as will you, my love, whom yet
I do not know but I already mourn.

(1975)

Cry Help

Cry help? You'll find me fast in my grave first
Who now could come if I did call
since our stronghold our hope our legitimate lord
has himself suffered seizure and failed?

Spun by the rip my mainstay snapped
arse breached with shit bile eats my gut
to see our ground our shelter our wildness our civilized precincts
hocked for a pittance by wasters

Our rivers their frets and divisions stand still
black marshes and palace the Bride and the Boyne
lake sound run red and the ominous seas
since that jack took the tricks from our king

Keen rain
on the road unsettles me
no sound comes near but the roar
of that unstoppable falls

Proud master of salient and hollow of royal demesnes
his stomach is lost with his lands
now the hawk who holds fast those rents and accounts
knows no man as kin

Come down too far from original heights
temporal races fret rockface
where raging headsprings supplement
the river that drops through the settlements

I stop and Death rides up to me
and the dragons are quenched in their courses
and I'm bound to follow my leader down
where His white ledger covers all the deal

(*For Brian Coffey*, 1992)

Cold Course

The jaded sun lies low in his halt galaxy,
set hard like honey in the stiff comb,
with house and planet, tree and shivering peregrine,
all subjects under him consepulchred,
underfoot and done for, a mere smoke of stars.
The August heat, geometry of dance, full wilt
and fall: all yet survive in the slow sugars;
so, he now sits throned in dust, holds
vestiges and memoranda for his court,
whose armies dominate their night
quicksilver courses irrigate.
These he thought measures to kill time and grief.
Gorged on vermilion, his peers sweated
bright death, transfused the rockveins to their own.
The sovereign they bolted down still circulates
through this enchanted fastness of white sudden stone.

(1990)

from Love Songs from a Dead Tongue

(Worked from the Middle Irish)

Kells, occasion for blindness,
since I lay with your king;
Kells, grown disfigured
now Niall is gone.

The first kings I wived,
I augmented their glory,
but Niall was far dearer than both;
Kells, occasion for blindness.

My bright Niall ceased,
my man and my king ceased,
here his broad lands continue;
Kells, occasion for blindness.

Well I remember generous Niall
here on this hill
laughing his wealth away;
Kells, occasion for blindness.

I will walk to the grave of Niall;
there is room where he lies
for me to lie next him;
Kells, occasion for blindness,
                                    blindness.

Here the hound is neglected
till proven,
the unloved
easily slighted.

The crow's black, say I say,
then, white, they say back;
I go wrong, the same say,
whether striding or bowed.

Bleak the hill without trees,
chill the shoulder unfriended,
and empty the weave without issue,
here, don't I know it?

As she finds in love
from one man satisfaction,
no he ever found
but one woman could please.

That king, son of kings, was my pleasure,
most loved and most brave, that most gentle man
stood head against head
with this child of the arch-king.

I a long age since
in this fort of crude strength,
my force fragile, this frail I,
can't abide
        here.

Wretched to me
my own homeland,
I'd sooner stay in Ulster
conversing with kings.

Through seventeen years
among this aristocracy
they have dealt with me kindly,
rather kinsfolk than strangers.

I and the mountain lark,
of a muchness our nature:
with the wood within reach
she sleeps in the peat-bog.

Getting so much from Niall
what reason to leave him?
that gentle slender-handed man,
unequalled.

[This development is obscure.]

....
        wretched.

(*For George Hitching*, 2002)

The Roads, People, the River
(Soured with Industrial Excrement) & Town:

What more reason for a bird's rapture
than in the silent passage of quiet people
whose dark labyrinth only comprehends them:

first night of spring; the wind
is white and full, the moon
is only a direction, without edges
or exact location in this long fall;

a radio speaks in a window's mouth
and it is not for such verbed symbols
working across the road's dumb ceaseless fall
their weave, their patterned maze,

that the beggar's hands are veined with lead,
his body without redolence of lilies,
nor that some windows lack familiar light now,
and flowers must be found, even in such snow;

by the distillery wall the vagrant's breath
grips on the frozen stone, the moon
is the white bird on his shoulder;
as sound, presence and colour, dragging

like golden ants upon their backs their own apprehension,
flock into his skull and make their nest, and breed,
what more reason for a bird's rapture?

(1969)

'93/4

In the closing days of 1993 my library and other traps were
delivered to my new lodgings near Kilcrea, Co. Cork

I've got no means of knowing for sure
if you can hear the knocking of the bells
as you anticipated from your open door
or just the slight hiss of the rain as here

this low cover that confounds all clarity
blocks from you too the hunter and the hounds
coursing in vain the high frost
from the zenith past this pitch past me

unthinking since at six I left you I've traversed
one entire quadrant of the sky
Algol ever duplicitous
salted your mine with stars as she swung by

since no-one's fixed your street-light there
that shorted in the recent storms
it's way too chancy now to call
the corner phone hoping you'd hear

but do my dear friend remember
to feed the fire I built
to counteract the streaming flood
inside your walls the spreading rot

here as the year turns over
anxious and half-insensible
with too much solitary alcohol
I stoke my own fire up

just a little on from that hard school
where dull O'Laoghaire learns at length
without either civility or song
the full weight of the heavy earth

I rise at intervals to welcome one
by one my new arrivals in
on boards of smooth white deal
for your pleasure I arrange

Dickinson and Dogen
Lorca and Tao Qian
with other esoterica
and miscellaneous pots and pans

my telescope leans blind against the wall
its mirror cataracted with fresh dust
lens unadjusted from the cloudy moon
we renounced last night

to set at large
the confined hour when hand
of thigh belly of head
make good sense unforeseen

now for a spell
the dead-headed
demon's carried
below the pole

it's high time to play again
with this present you devised
with care locate
your traces in the volatile oils

rosewood lavender and ceaseless
rosemary release their essential
and complex vapours
above the steady flame

that in the column of the lamp
burns almost enclosed
aware the unfinished buddha
at the shut summit

of the terraced worlds
sees the rough suns tumble out
where the furious high god
hurls his net

and each jewelled node
glitters with every other
as they fall
effortless exactly

through the empty now
let's together each
again make free
for the time being

that is not nothing

(1995)

To-do

The door is in bits
fix it forthwith
eggshells and light
to make weight

Such a high and dry
pass between quarters
you walked through me
like rain

You can't trust that stair
tread it
with feathers with scum
underfoot

The king
must go up now
his desolate angels
have gone

The gate slams abandoned
tether it tie it
with sand with great care
against strangers

Hand and tongue
can undo
what hard days and dark glamour
have joined

The bridge is back-broken
so splint it
with girders of salt and with laughter
at tides

Along thoroughfares
closed for repair

we knew ghosts to go hungry
saw the halt waters walk

The causeway comes round
again round
again round
again

leave it

(*For Tina*, 1995)

once encountered
you will always
know the tormentil

deep the mineral
soil is scaled
and red with iron

pines are dense
and acidlogged

fresh rains
run rancid
in the level
dark

and raise
the yellow
tormentil

(2007)

the marvellous
bird
won't sing
on every
branch

i don't
always have
a quilted
bed

pity me
wait for me
turn to me
kiss me
pity me

red apple
eating
straw bale
sleeping

turn to me

(2007)

let's have
a market
in affects

bulls
gravitate
to rage
bears to
disproportionate
sadness

shorts
considering
happiness
overvalued
are active
there

options
offer
profits
with
significant
risk

secondary
markets
trading
used
securities
are deep
and abject

(2007)

eye
masked
behind
its own
force

mouth issuing
fears and agitated
reminiscence
through which
both threats
and pleadings
are sensible

fists beating
feet pacing body
twisted between
vehement
extremities

ah yes

you are
trafficking
in feelings

(2007)

Saws

1

flame has a skin of cold
light sets limit to the dark
so name me then
the outside rind of memory
the clothes love wears

•

rock in the streambed
fluid thats your element is absence
complex with vortices and currents
bears cold against the bone
still hand reaches grips itself

•

silence vexed
touch when presence would suffice
anatomizing scrutiny
break the made whole
care gathers mute blind here

•

faulting crowd from fend
touch impairs the waist the small
the shoulder prompts the touch
as instruments diminish even to the heart
needs must intents persist

•

spontaneously sight unseen
in the intervals between
where venture hunts its gain
beasts may become familiar
and grow tame

2

hold friends and colours and sleep fast
inch an abyss ocean no barrier
truly the execution is woeful
passion suffers where the flimsy heart
wont break wont break

•

chance set of winds you
fixed deck of bones you
my chambered and mined
my furnished with tables
my table of cases of tides

•

the water touched
deteriorates and gains
last of whats passing
first of whats to come
robs and returns

•

action dons habit of effect
sleight uncontrolled
ghosted out from us
how ever to come to again
if we nothing have laid down

•

every sake acknowledged serves
this am traversed by words
provisional coherence
interim and out of sorts
able for joy

3

mirrors eclipses departures
loss instantaneous or slow
barren doubling
death is all we see awake
and sleeping only sleep

•

fronts and systems move across
through the weather of such data
drifting hungers and accessory rage
you claim with care your personal effects
as general consequence accrues

•

no cage is found for wind or rain
so older than desire that stirs the hand
prior to relief to grief to nerve and nerves
what by the heart
is hidden hidden is

•

structures unseen the seen decide
you near space intervenes
gone head will conjure head the lid the lip
waking we share and sleeping turn aside
eyes twinned make the world deep

•

have you forgotten
that past is anyhow indelible
scape from its map withdraws
to lodge at heart in dream through fright flight poised
map gone you have forgotten nothing

(*For Linda*, 2001)

Chimaera

Ceres and Bacchus bid good night
sharp frosty fingers all your flowers have topped
and what scythes spared winds shave off quite

    a moth bred out of moonlight I disturbed
    from the dark folds where it lay hid

        a naked thing that seems no man may cheat
        and love like any jack
        another dressed may prove a beast

        that creature fluttered free but voided in my lap
        a maggot with a human head monstrous misshapen

such whose white satin upper coat of skin
cut upon velvet rich incarnadin
has yet a body and of flesh within

        whereas anything with six foot of skeleton
        with hands that grip with scalp of hair
        front teeth concealed inside a face
        and which leans forward as it runs
        is called a man with us

the joys of earth and air are thine entire
that with thy feet and wings dost hop and fly

    the sky unrolled its folds of purple and blue to the winds
    and later from these steps I saw on the horizon
    a village torched by soldiers blaze like a comet in the sky

then ah the sickle golden ears are cropped
dropping December shall come weeping in

        the blood of horses become jack o lantern
        the blood of men become will o the wisp
        kites become sparrow hawks and those hawks cuckoos

when the sun opened its golden lashes on the chaos of worlds
and the earth was adrift with its cargo of ashes and bones
my terrified soul then fled through the grey web of halflight
but that spawn hung on in this shrill rush
and spun himself into the full of its white mane

     cuckoos in due course again turn raptor
     swallows become oysters seashells hatch geese

poor verdant fool and now green ice thy joys
large and as lasting as thy perch of grass
bid us lay in gainst winter rain and poise

     apes grown of sheep fish that are rotten fruit
     flies born of roe such transformations are

     souls of the dead like mountain oaks uprooted by demons
     souls of the dead like meadow flowers gathered by angels
     sun sky earth man all had begun all gone

I cannot tell who loves the skeleton
of a poor marmoset naught but bone bone

(*For Tina Murphy*, 1995)

light
astral
obdurate
implacable

light
the strongest
biggest
thing

crouch
down here
beside me
light my pet
my little dog
my doll

and i will
caress
untangle your
wild hair
and you will
be my
friend

(2005)

examine
your own
features your
distinguishing
characteristics

are you so
sleek?

pelt
cannot
remain
intact
eye
always
bright

living
dims

here we
enhance
the vestiges
of animation

with wire
and common
glass
we mend
broken
beasts

(*For Jessica Jones*, 2007)

Hopeful Monsters

Phases of the eye agitated through wings

When my great ancestor succeeded to the throne, there appeared just a phoenix at that time. Thereupon, he took birds for his reign, making bird-officers and using the elaborate insignia of birds, recognizing that whereas with the common hen after three days and three nights there is the first indication of the embryo, with more intricate birds the interval is longer, slight with the exhausted.

Meanwhile, when first the heart appeared like a speck of blood in the white of the egg, the Phoenix Master was appointed to arrange the calendar, and the Dark Bird Master to balance day with night. The Shrike Master undertook the solstice, because this point beats and moves as though endowed with life, and from it twin vein-ducts fraught with blood trend in a convoluted course, and a membrane carrying bloody fibres very swiftly envelops the yolk, leading off from the vein-ducts.

He had from the beginning an inner and an outer sphere with a north pole and south pole, an ecliptic, the equator, twenty-four positions of the sun during the year, twenty-eight lunar stations, the sun, moon, the five planets, the inner and outer stars, from which, the head being clearly distinguished, and in it the eyes, swollen out to a great extent, it was only by degrees that they diminished and collapsed. The whole was moved by water-power and placed in an upper room of the palace.

When the egg was aged ten days the chick and all its components were distinctly visible. The head was still larger than the rest of the body, and the eyes larger than the head, but still devoid of vision. Simultaneously it set in motion a wheel of fortune, whatever that was, and in front of the steps of the palace there was a monthly flower, which, conformably to the waxing and waning of the moon, every day had a new blossom or dropped one. The eyes, if removed during sleep, were found to be larger than beans and black, and, the cuticle being peeled back from them, there was discovered a white and cold liquid inside, quite glittering in the sunlight, but no hard substance whatsoever. And they said to me: He won't mind, just for a little while, will you? He will sit here, and see the squirrel run round in his treadmill.

About the twentieth day, if you had then opened the egg and touched the chick, it would have moved inside and chirped; and it was already coming to be covered with down, when, after the twentieth day was past, the beak began to break the shell. So long as the diurnal luminary was visible, then there was day, the head situated over the right leg close to the flank, and the wing placed over the head. When it vanished and the nocturnal luminary took its place, we had night, and he examined then the gem-adorned turning sphere, and the gem transverse tube, that he might regulate the seven Directors.

By this time it was growing darker, and nearly dark. It was a perfectly strange room to me; for there had been so much in it to engross my attention, that I had looked about me scarcely at all. There was now, however, nothing left but to look about me. You will understand that with the waxing and waning moon the brains of animals, the marrow of bones and trees, and the flesh of crabs and snails grow and shrink together. There were several cages, occupied, ranged against the wall; but, with the exception of a blackbird, all the birds were asleep, with their heads under their wings – still as balls of feathers. The blackbird was still, too, all but his eyes, which winked and blinked at me whenever I turned my gaze that way.

There were, besides the blackbird and the squirrel, a whale's tooth on the sideboard, and a great-bellied jug with a man's head, with the mouth wide open for a spout. The Green Bird Master was at once assigned the inception, and the Carnation Bird Master the completion of the seasons, but the darker it grew, the stranger everything seemed to get, and bigger and bigger the blinking eyes of the blackbird, till I was afraid to look about me at all, and kept my eyes fixed on the squirrel's cage on the table, with the little squirrel within spinning round and round in his wire wheel. During the period above referred to the chick slept, woke up, moved fretfully and looked up and chirped; and the heart and navel together palpitated as though the creature were respiring.

The great clock in the corner had ticked off very many more than a few minutes. It was quite dark now; and I could see nothing of the squirrel but the white patch on his breast, ever shifting, and rising and falling behind the bright bars of his prison, as he whirled it swiftly round. When I say that this was all I could see, I mean to say that it was all I tried to see. Had I looked about, no doubt I should have found the blackbird's eyes bigger and fuller of winks than ever; and, possibly, the big-bellied man-jug champing his jaws at me. This looks very much like a later embellishment. There was plenty to listen to, however. There was the creaking of the squirrel's wheel, and the clawing of its feet; there was the ticking of the great clock; and plain above the ticking, and the creaking, and the clawing, a dull tramping overhead.

The final step was to examine a wide variety of substances, paper, ashes, red lead, gold, silver, copper, grass, blue flowers, bubbles of water tinged with various colours, peacock's feathers and such like. Under red light, all showed red, under blue light, blue, under green, green and so on. For my part, the bullfinch gave me enough to think of. By the dull light of the moon I had been able to make out little more than its mere shape. Now, however, it was plainly revealed from its head to its tail. It was death itself, and so I regarded it. My eyes were drawn towards it, and would not be withdrawn, for when the sun and moon are being eaten, does not one help them? Its black, eyeless, bullet-shaped head; its wide agape beak; its straddle legs; the crimson blurs and smirches that stained its body; the bright, sharp wires which trussed it in every direction, fascinated my gaze completely. The instrument was made of copper and deeply fatigued.

An assistant in a closed room had to take notice of all the changes, and to call out to an observer on a high tower whether a star on the sphere was just appearing, culminating, or disappearing. Presently the dwindling candle began to sputter, and its flame to gasp for breath, as it were – rising and falling like a man that is drowning, and seeming to make the spitted bird rise and fall, and to wriggle and writhe to get free from the spikes in it. Then, with a struggle, I turned my face to the wall, and falling asleep, never awoke. The motions of the instrument were in exact accordance with the motions of the heavens.

Damaged, we bleed time

A body thrown vertically down from the top of a tower moves through a distance of 88 feet during the third second of its flight. Calculate, then, the speed of projection, and determine the speed at which the sleeve begins to move upwards.

Furthermore, here take note of the exact proportions of a man. Those of a woman will I disregard, for she has no set proportion but her history: that of a middle-aged female seen by the police waiting on the side of the bridge where they have much to learn yet concerning the depths, almost wholly unexamined as they are, and covering three-fourths of the surface.

When he attempted to speak to her, the patient jumped, falling some 30 feet into about 20 feet of water. There is always a chance therefore that the critical act or change may take place when the observer's eyes are withdrawn. Mild plethora of the face ensued, it being divided into three parts, namely: the forehead, fair complected, one; the nose, another, sand present in abundance there admixed with small crustacean shells; and from the nose to chin, exhibiting extensive tooth loss though with roots intact, another. Notice the blood tinged fluid coming from the mouth. Red is warm and radiates across the ground.

From the side of the nose through the whole length of the eye, one of these measures, as also from the end of the eye up to the ear. Seeing this, immediately he called the rescue squad, who quickly discovered the patient floating facedownward in a water whose tides consisted of a series of superimposed undulations. Not only are there the ordinary semi-diurnal tides caused by sun and moon, but a series of minor tides, such as the lunar diurnal, the solar diurnal, the lunar monthly, the lunar fortnightly, the solar annual and the solar semi-annual, which each impede or augment the course of years.

All this aside, it took about 15 minutes to get her out of the water by boat, whereupon she was noted to have dilated pupils. The simplest possible field of sight is like a white-washed wall: inarticulate, plain and motionless, as the chilled universe will find itself at the end of time. No pulse, no spontaneous respirations. Thus, unexplored tracts are gradually diminished. She was cold and modelled.

From one ear to the other, one face. From the chin under the jaw to the base of the throat, one measure.

On arrival, her temperature was noted to be 79.9° and still no pulse was seen in her, nor spontaneous respiration, just the monitor's flat line. At once she was intubated. The throat, lacking injuries to either hyoid or larynx, and in which the thyroid gland was observed to be small, was one measure long. From the pit of the throat to the top of the shoulder, one face; and so for the other shoulder. From the shoulder to the elbow, one face. From the elbow to the joint of the hand, of purple livor without track of needle, one face and one of the three measures. The whole hand, lengthwise, one face.

It may happen that we are not aware of all the conditions under which our researches are made. Some substance may be present or some power may be in action, which escapes the most vigilant examination. Not being aware of its existence, we are unable to take proper measures to exclude it, and thus determine the share which it has in the results of our experiments. So, we cannot deny even the strange suggestion of Young, that there may be independent worlds, some possibly existing in different parts of space, but others perhaps pervading each other unseen and unknown in the same space.

Proceeding, then, from the pit of the throat to that of the chest, or stomach, which held about an egg-cupful of mucoid liquid, black to burgundy in colour, was one face. Heart: 360 grams. From the navel to the thigh joint, one face. From the thigh to the knee, two faces. From knee to heel of leg, two faces.

The foot was one face long, and all extremities were clean, with nails of moderate length. There was, however, a gauze dressing present on the dorsum of the right foot, and some cyanosis of the nailbeds. Just so, a latch-key may look lazy or aggressive, opening on a field once inundated, sown and harvested, now grazed by clocks, dull unproductive beasts grinding and eliminating all as one, or, further back, upon the creaks, groans, screams, thunderclaps and drumrolls of our own sun's song where iron is the final ash of nuclear burning.

Those which resembled each other in shape, size, direction, colour, brightness, or location clustered at the eye. IVs were started and warming measures instituted. The patient's pH was noted to be 7.69. She was warm to 98.6° by rectal probe. In more than one case the unsuspected presence of common salt in the air has caused great trouble. Brain weight 1250 grams; mildly congested; no lesions.

A man having no cavity blood or effusions, nor recent fractures to the axial skeleton, is as long as his arms crosswise. Those arms, hands included, reach to the middle of the thigh, which very hands may discover things not seen, hiding under the shadow of natural objects, and fix them in plain sight, rendering to the sense what does not actually exist. The whole man is eight faces and two of the three measures in length, and he has one breast rib less than a woman, on the left side. She, for her part, had still no response to any interventions, despite the dryness of both lungs, and the absence of lesions on the urinary bladder, which was empty.

A man has several bones in all, and beauty is lost when meaning and form are split asunder. The handsome man must be swarthy, and the woman fair, etc., the genitalia, both internal and external, without injury. Provisional diagnosis: probable drowning. And had we exhausted all the known phenomena of a mechanical problem, how could we tell that hidden phenomena, as yet undetected, do not intervene in the commonest actions? I will not speak to you about the irrational animals, because you will never discover any system of proportion in them.

Scene preserved with light crazing

The joy of being tamed is greatest in those animals that lie longest with their parents and are most grievously associated with them, for do not all fixed bodies, heated, shed soft light? The young of predators, even those not hungry, invariably shriek and howl when left alone, withering when protection is withdrawn and dreading solitude, however tenderly near bodies of water and earth may gleam when sufficiently agitated by heat, by friction, percussion, putrefaction, or any other cause, for since it is heavy with dependence, the filial sentiment is particularly ready to accept a substitute. The practical qualities a governor must possess are, therefore, (1) sensitiveness, (2) effort and power, and (3) stability. The significance of these will be explained in several paragraphs.

The public executioner provides mutilated criminals (foot-amputees are particularly mentioned) to guard the preserve, recognizing that neither love nor hatred, kindness nor cruelty are any more connected with the fundamental impulses that move us than with chemical reactions. Evidently the royal preserves are not pure enclaves of wilderness, protected though they be from unauthorized intrusions, as for instance, sea-water in a raging storm; the back of a cat or neck of a horse obliquely struck or rubbed in a dark place; wood, flesh and fish while they putrefy; vapours arising from rotting waters; stacks of moist hay or corn grown alien by fermentation; glow-worms and the eyes of certain animals; the vulgar phosphorus suffering intense attrition; amber and some diamonds struck, pressed or rubbed; iron hammered very nimbly till it become so hot as to kindle sulphur thrown upon it; until on one memorable occasion, the axletrees of chariots taking fire by the rapid rotation of the wheels, they roasted a foreign shaman within the Supreme Forest.

These all enter into the composition of what we speak of as 'love', which, as Spencer says, fuses into one immense aggregate most of the elementary excitations of which we are capable. So deeply faulted a sentiment may well become a dominant inspiration of foreboding and of art, and in order to increase the sensitiveness, either the frictional resistances of the governor mechanism and the regulating gear must be reduced, or since desire cannot be entirely eliminated, the power of the governor must be increased. This is most easily effected by loading the governor by means of a dead weight.

One remote territory sent a gold-sifting bird as tribute. Men said that its home was beyond even the burning island. This bird is shaped like a sparrow, but its colour is yellow. Feathers and interruption are soft and fine. It usually swoops and soars above the sea. When a netsman gathers one he takes it to be the outcome of dreamings. Hearing the virtue of our King spread far over the wildernesses, they accordingly traversed mountains and navigated seas to bring one to him, which he at once dispatched to the Garden for Numinous Fowl, providing it true pearl for sweetmeat and turtle brain for drink. It is no irrelevance that this bird regularly spits up gold powder like millet grain, which may be cast to make utensils.

Wishing to prove that oxygen is necessary to life, however, we do not settle a broody hen within a vessel exhausted by burning. We should then have not only an absence of oxygen, but subtle residues of flame might prove the destructive agent. By attending to a clutch of chickens from birth, drawing them outward through interlocking shells of light and transformation, one experimenter completely ousted their mother, and the chicks would, without any encouragement, follow him everywhere without taking the slightest notice of their own bereaved parent. In every case, therefore, there is a time-lag between the change of governor configuration and the regulation of power.

Such sentiments fresh in my mind, this morning I showed the King those young children which we had preserved, and as the secretion in other flowers sometimes takes place rapidly and might occur at early dawn, that inconvenient hour of observation was specially adopted. The one was a male infant about 4 months, who was cut out of a woman's belly in Covent Garden (she was dying of a consumption) and had been (now four years past) luted up in a globe of glass about 8 or 10 inches in diameter, set nicely in a frame where it may be swiftly spun upon its axis, shining where it rubs the outreached hand, the babe within preserved from putrefaction by a liquor of our special making. The flesh was not so much rumpled but plump as it was when taken out of the womb, and in rushing out of the glass will sometimes push against the finger so as to be felt. The other was 2 girls joined together by the breast and belly (which monster was born about the king's coming in), they were dried, preserved with spices, and flowers of different ages were subjected to irritant vapours, to moisture, and to every condition likely to bring on the secretion. Only after invariable failure of this exhaustive inquiry was the barrenness of nature assumed proved in this instance.

This cycle of events is repeated and gives rise to periodic fluctuations of speed known as hunting. Do, please, try to remember this. Animals are preying being; the perception of a mangled, bleeding, or of a suffering, weak, and helpless creature means to the universal disposition of animal life a prey, food. That the suffering animal belongs to the same species, or is a close associate, makes no difference. Hunting is not, however, solely associated with isochronous governors.

About 9 o'clock I acquainted the King with my discovery of Irish lands, whose gracious answer was that what I desired should be done. "When Indians have killed a cow buffalo," says one authority, "the calf follows them and licks their hands." A man dies on the day which he has always regarded as his last, from his own fears of the day. An incantation effects its purpose, because care is taken to frighten the intended victim, by letting him know his fate. In all cases the mental condition is the cause of apparent coincidence. The manner in which the domestication of animals first took place will be apparent from such instances, and you may easily now proceed to demonstrate how a simple governor may be made nearly isochronous by crossing the arms.

Plates of various material, such as rough iron, glass, polished metal, exposed to the midnight sky, though indestructible as honey, will be dewed in various degrees. When the royal party arrived, the events began. A shrewd wind of feathers, a rain of blood, sprinkled the countryside, covered the sky. Until the knife tire of the milk, figures will find their ground.

(*For Angela*, 1998)

Elegy of the Shut Mirror

Inside rooms I've never seen
an old man beats himself
at chess, the moon recurs
as a white dove in a child's dream,
a virgin leaves the glass
and, turning the light, retires;
as the mirror broods on itself.

Though the sun burns still through a vacant sky
frost thickens on the gates
and the moon grows up in the poplar's shade.

A girl waits, lonely, on the bridge.
can I tell her of remote roads
where love, not knowing the shock of loss,
has atrophied, and no-one sees
how, at the desolate junctions
the monuments of the old dead bleed
with the green ichors of bronze;

or there are streets,
icy now where pools contract,
where I have heard the ringing footfalls of a child
who will remember evenings
charged with light, fever
of strange games played
in the falling of the oblique sun;
the private hurt of times and words
not uttered yet.

And shall I tell the destitute
how I have found their misery
like the wardrobe of a suicide, where I
the living, recognize
only the faded linens, the frayed cloth,
the torn letters in an inside pocket,
extracts from an unintelligible
and unfinished history;

or tell the old of aging
and the inevitable death.
with dusk the rain comes;
the ice loosens and the expanding locks
respond and open. such time impedes
the passage of another fall
that drags through lengthening nights
into the season of its bitter end.

(1970)

Neglect in Camera

It is another obscure chamber. The town is trapped in light and shade, and limited to the back wall of the shop. The glasses man and his parrot inhabit an intermediate dimension.

The parrot knows the names of things. *Roskyn,* he says. Then, *shag, cendal, gazzatum, dobby, fleece.* An ignorance of grammar does not allow his speech to accumulate meaning. His master draughts the projected image on his scrim. Things he knows, but not their names.

They make an odd pair, this glasses man and his pet. When the bird dies, his master will have him stuffed, he loves him so. Already selected is the corner in which he will perch, steadfast. The figures moving through the inverted silver town are averaged into a poised stasis. They represent the citizens as the bird represents the tropics.

Later, the glasses man will attend with oils to the precise textures of cloth, of hair, of milk pouring, a needle penetrating lace, sunlight on pearl, on skin. His nails are dark from years of grinding colours. His eyes are dark from years. His skin? *Gossamer!*

(2007)

Spring Comes

past scope of silk
stirrup and bow
undergo refinement
as incoherence
regulates the sands

Scene vividly displays, in a mild transform of the received,
Flowering branches penetrate throughout the ancient yet intact.
Courts and corridors, row on row, are solemn, majestic and impressive,
Green tiles load the eaves, terraced pavilions cancel curious eyes.

Conserved together, one hundred and nine people appearing lifelike,
At different ages have distinguished identities, tics, composures;
Gestures and actions are varied, whether at flowers or holding things;
Laughter at birds' play by the veranda, then haste smart coach to the midyard.

Consorts are ensembling the bamboo flute, drum, pipe and chime stone;
Engrossed at chess some ponder, while others more at ease are dressing;
Some enjoy fish, tease parrots, paint long recessions of unbolted doors;
Harness and armour glint at the gate, generals bow, reign in their hearts.

Varied posture and colour of the imperial concubines
In bright peaceful and happy deluxe like we like;
Luminosity so intense night will plunder,
Awkward dark stranger, uncouth invader. Mercy!

Clustered peonies, towering pines, peacocks in glorious exhibition
And red-crowned crane shouting at each other;
Purple camel-humps seethe agreeably in viridian glaze;
All is blended, and implied meanings are deep, implicit and rather fascinating.

Composition is exquisite, layout clearly demarcated.
It gives a splendid scene of the gentle people echoing and clustering.
The plot of false or true, moving or still, has been organically linked.
Truly monstrates natural interaction, is worth seeing a hundred times.

(*For Geoffrey Squires*, 2007)

Two Songs from the Hungarian

Father, come home,
my mother's not well.
Hold on, daughter,
I'm dancing.

Father, come home,
my mother's being shrived.
Hold on, daughter,
I'm dancing.

Father, come home,
my mother is dead.
Hold on, daughter,
I'm dancing.

Father, come home,
my mother's being waked.
Hold on, daughter,
I'm dancing.

Father, come home,
my mother's being buried.
Hold on, daughter,
I'm dancing.

Katy falls sick
by the walnut trees,
by the hazel trees,
by the nut-tree grove.

Her mother asks her
where's the pain.
Not my head,
not my heart.

My head
doesn't hurt,
my heart
doesn't hurt.

Mother have my heart
cut out,
my calling heart,
my joy.

Have it cut out,
pack it up in a case
and carry it safe
to the shop.

When they ask you
what you sell,
say it's Katy's calling heart,
her joy.

(2007)

DARK SENSES PARALLEL STREETS

bones show through images   more opaque than tissue
of friends though they   strut pressured between joints
still move in dialogue   with tongue blades fluttering
in darkness what relief   to accumulate some utterance

forgive me it's a dream   don't mention it
standing alone waving   it's easy to be fooled
in search of its lost era   rich spoils
not just geography   forgotten in the foreclosed mine

walking parallel streets   try to conceive the waste
of tropical flames   blossoming from the settled earth
with a political broom   to suppress the outburst
ominous as a smoke signal   you needn't understand

over a farewell meal   make smalltalk avoid disturbance
of dust in the dust   breath lays down
before an open window   another field of vision
weather permitting   in clarity precedent to the rain

step sharply within   no time to lose here
the labyrinth of raw meat   though deepening fatigue
jingling those keys   won't achieve much you know
dimmed by sweat   regrettably the outlines just blur

unthinking insects click rustle   case on case scavenging
for bare subsistence   replicate the given circulating minutes
in the skeletons of organizations   to the extremities
inexorably crushed by vice   the central pump stutters

they themselves go into hiding   in heavy concentrations
one on top of another   level obliterates level
in their natural colours   exhibiting an astonishing mimicry
green smocks masks and goggles   rendering discrimination vain

taking likenesses   vow to represent all valid subjects
to build a screen   transfix each distinct stage
alongside the trail   ideal ghost doll exactly fashioned
of pearl lightbulb shards   reaching back to darkness

this curiously shaped barrier   bonding fine with foul
contains gestures and rites   offends memory and ambition
simulated leopard skins   such odd effects are collateral
smart cards and our ideas   of no account

for fear of disturbing   the familiar infirm ground
the pose of philosophy   is an exhausted problem
fashionable at the time   their expressions were captured
they stand in complete silence   reduced to immobility

in unbroken sunlight   an extended field of whiteness
wearing masks   to encompass each their private night
as aids to memory   for elaborating dark senses
attributed to interiors unknown   byproducts of hidden systems

they did not break   the established building regulations
under their own weight   level bearing level down
the experience of generations   supporting the cumulative moment
proved far more effective   with a dense stratification

acts of representation respond   in manifold discrete effects
in order to survive desire   endure recurring visitations
cheated by false hopes   concentrating an intense violence
in voices hardly above a whisper   phrases disfigure

local weather prophets   invoke the movements of fronts
proclaim their laws of storm   against the individual
radioactive rain restricted   storm raging in a cell
to areas over toxic waste   possessed of spoil

the nightmare atmosphere of ruin   admitting sensory leakage
washes away in close-up   what could you expect
striking spatial effects predicted   to attract all comers
if the mask is joyful   after so much

produce a sublime gesture   when several significant figures
opposed to voice or action   question whether pleading
a system of reflections ordering   direct and material interest
the necessity of ornament   can openly be countenanced

(*With & for Tom Raworth*, 2000)

o tiny
universe

alongside
the many other
possible
universes
some of which
could easily
be ten
or a thousand
times more
vast

you are
small
pretentious
and a little
pathetic

i will
keep you
for later

(2005)

always
different
isn't it?

even though
you sketch
the structure
beforehand

even after all
childhood spent
aloft or dreaming
outbursts
of limbs

branching
surprises

and always
from the highest
twig
the redbreast
calls you
sweetly
up

(*For Marrie Mooij*, 2007)

a complete
world

trees
beasts
birds
and men

is realized
in whiteness

cool blue
white
of the pruning
peasant

cream of the
milking
herdsman

fleece
of a different
blank
again

the wind
is in the sky

(2007)

not all
plants
are alike

some are
astringent
some are
salty

some sour
some sweet

some men
are short
-lived
some long

some ugly
others fortunate

weak strong
stupid clever
poor rich

was it
brevity
you wanted?

(2007)

De Iron Trote

As man, in deep and level sleep, periodically draws a long inspiration, song is learned and figured in the brain. Think of the way a musical box, wound up, potentially represents a slow or lively air.

Clothes, however thick, diminish little the sonorities of breath. Touch the stop and the air sounds out; send an impulse along the proper afferent nerve and voice starts on song. Succussion, too, may raise a splashing sound much like the respiration, voice, and tinkling. Odd.

Garments of silk, or thin dry wool, also give rise to a noise calculated to cause error, sometimes mitigating the production and carefully controlled cropping of live creatures for high ends. Else, from every corner of the woods and glens see them come creeping on their hands, for their legs cannot make fast, as in humans the larynx migrates down the neck since the age of eighteen months, from which arises the sound of voices. In time these come to speak of a political meeting, of market shares. Someone tells of a woman who murdered her lover. "A chauffeur kills his wife," says another. All teetotallers like sugar. No nightingale drinks wine. Go figure.

The respiration of the plumpest child is louder clothed than of the thinnest adult frame stripped down. The throat is delicate and worthy to be protected. Says who? Whose voice? What proof is there these brutes are other than a superior race of marionettes, which eat without pleasure, cry without pain, desire nothing, know nothing, merely simulating true intelligence, for all it has been said that when emotions stir within, they take form in words?

To be included here is the agopithecus, an ape-like goat whose voice is very like a man's but not articulate, sounding as if one did speak hastily with indignation or sorrow, as here, where one such encounters in the woods a boy: "What's that you have?" The boy holds it out. It is a toy, a bear. A teddy bear. The boy's eyes are large, but without expression. "I don't want it, keep it." The boy hugs the bear again. A house takes fire. Later comes the writing of authorizations and designs on shop window tickets, and of inscriptions too private to allow printing.

In women who are both grown up and fat, the respiration is often audible with great force, even through the breasts. When your raptors are at fault, prevent all speech: let such as follow them ignorantly and unworthily, stirrup all aloof, for whilst such are chattering, none will hunt. *A-propos*,

Sir, a politician will say: "What news from America?" *A-propos*, "Do you think both the admirals will be tried?" Or, *a-propos*, "Did you hear what has happened to my grandmother?"

Such rustling sensations are nothing else than a purring-thrill, and when this co-exists with the sound of the bellows, rasp, or file we may be assured others will soon resemble anatomies of death, like ghosts crying out of their graves, and will eat the dead carrions, happy where they find them, and the very carcasses they spare not to scrape back out of their deeper sleep.

Ticket writers may proceed to designs for posters when they can name their own figure. The illusion of experience, as a rule, begins by filling in provided letters with paint, and later gets on to the proper writing and lettering. Attendance at technical classes would be useful in order to bring up a good style of writing with some originality.

A dull but strong sound like that produced by a file on wood has something harsh in its sound. So, other boys start as heaters, then exercise as rivet-carriers, holders-up, anvil-hands, and lastly platers. Hear the whizzing sound of the left auricle.

Caution: Boys are often required to stand inside the chamber, as supp-orters, while the men pierce, and then hammer it outside, and deafness is apt to result. I found one who had abandoned his laborious occupation, and gained an easy place as servant to a priest.

Work with letters may be done sitting without difficulty and is quite suitable for cripples. The trade is not a large one.

In order
        to succeed
                a boy
should have a
        taste
                for drawing

ties
        with wild
                designs

unrestrained
    by thumb-
        tacks,

and thereby
    put by
        for a secure
old age
    a tidy
        sum,

for he might yet
    have to pit
        a warrant
'gainst a blackjack,
    drag
        his doll

with teats
    hitched,
        not as the fastidious
permit,
    but heaved
        in fullest view

by a snurting,
    as if some crack
        ensemble
had outrageously
    let
        fly

against all
    refined
        precedent
when we would have
    some prudence
        hinder her.

"Rear
      exit and begone,
           my own
exhibitionistic pet!
      Let's catch
           the track

will lead us
      to our train
           of state,
then venerably
      process."
           "A chorus

we must have
      to free ourselves
           of drills
and drawbacks,
      trials
           and tribulations."

Experience
      will seize
           the way.
Don't fix
      what ain't yet broke.
           You've heard it's true

that by a snifting
      clack
           the air
is expelled
      from the
           pickle-pot.

(*For Keith Tuma*, 2003)

128

Pentahedron

I   In the soft dark rain
the presence of the sleeping man
is sensed only by dogs.
they scent and whine.

Stars have grown up in the sky like fruit,
the moon corrodes, the moon
falls like ash and smoulders;
sourness of acid rain.

When your lips are falling through the ruined jaw
they will remember autumn
and the painful fruit.

Go now into the central squares
(prison of statues, great as trees,
whose gestures spread above our heads
like branches through contorted air).

When your lips melt from the bone
and rats sip from your skull's trough
then they will fear the vagrant's dream,
recall his song.

The impregnable marble bodies;
in the rain the blind eyes weep.
again through close oppressive night
the soft beak nags the shell.

II   The way from school is across the bridge
where pregnant waters kiss green stone
and on the plinth where an old man sleeps
slogans of love dissolve.

Look where the sun has entered the canal
and summer decorates the railway track
quake-grass above the gentle moss
responds to tepid rain.

Torture of the word and understanding
pain of the flesh in song:
the mouth, unanswered, falls away,
sorrow,
          and the beat of rain.

Yet the sleeper does not wake.
in the narrow lanes by the cathedral
the air is motionless, and maybe
heavy with thunder.

An old man in a bed of stone
sees children, who dread
the sanity of unknown men,
stoning a sheep's head at the lock.

In the forest of the suspect eye they dance,
listen to the cripple's song.

III   Forest of grey cones dropping
    on an orange bed of wood;
    a ridge of pines, the river then,
    burying its silence and its empty foam
    and the firm blue bodies of its fish
    under a barren wall of stone.

    The fountains do not speak.
    their cherubs rot incessantly;
    battered truncated death.
    red sandstone falls to clay.

    It is not white water in the fountain's mouth,
    not volleying water; the moon plays on the velvet stone.

    You touch the sleeping body by the plinth;
    it falls in dust.

    Never the nail through the shattered wrist,
    never the body mad with fire,
    only the mouth clogged with soft ash
    breathing the reek of pain.

    The moon's corrosion hunts your face
    and your flesh grows sweet in the wasted air.
    when your lips are falling through the calcined wreck
    they will remember autumn;
                    time of fruit.

IV   This singing in the lilac.
          blackbirds. but the vaults are deaf,
          the loneliness. two girls
          in the cathedral garden
          have intimate knowledge and silence.

          Children playing on the ruined plots
          disturb tramps and loving youths.
          decay has forestalled demolition,
          old men are garrulous and drunk.

          Moons through the night sky fall,
          futility. in a deserted lane
          the moan of lovers from an upstairs room.
          poor sour despair. this guilt
          of needing bread to live.

          The thoroughfares and pubs are full,
          where all things move in their circle
          and all emotion has its root
          in misunderstanding.

          The loneliness. these two,
          their mutual remorselessness
          agile as the cripple's dream.
          this singing in the lilac;
          these blackbirds. this guilt.

V   I know these streets,
as crammed with dream as a clock with time;
yellow groundsel through the broken flags
grows into the mouths of children:
even the stone ages.

The blinds of the Jewish butcher's shop
are drawn.
          an old man dies.
his brain is full of curious dreams
of histories and of old men's deaths.

Hours elude the wheeling hands
but the ratchet locks return.

Light gathers in deserted streets,
dawn-light
          loose as yellow silk;
in the grain-littered yards of the distilleries
shadows of birds are born.

Though vagrants waken in familiar streets
and, still, the demented laugh in zones within the hospital,
children learn the early truths.
menaced by lights upon the wall
and feverish coughing from another room,
they stir in an uneasy sleep.
somewhere a violin, insomniac, speaks deep into the night.

This morning, in the Jewish quarter, and beyond,
merchants are abroad. the old
invent their lives again, coterminal, in shuttered rooms.

Unidentifiable cries stoop like a willow
over the hospital wall into the street I know.

(for Michael Smith, 1970, 1972)

STILLSMAN

I STILL THE HEART BEATS AS THE FIRST LIGHT BROACHES THE HORIZON
HUNDREDS OF BIRDS STRIKE UP THEIR TINY BODIES FILLING THE AIR
WITH FF MELODIES CUT WITH A SOLEMN OATH RECALL THE PATIENT
ONE OSCAR C THOUGH A BED FULL OF BONES HAD ALWAYS ENJOYED
EXCELLENT HEALTH PRESENTING NEVER BUT THE SHALLOWEST OF
MALADIES AND BEING NEITHER ALCOHOLIC NOR SYPHILITIC GREW
INTO A BRIGHT SHARP MAN POSSESSING THE THREE GIFTS OF HEARING
SEEING AND OF JUDGEMENT AND HAVING PERDURED LONG IN TEXTILES
HAD FOUND TRACTIBLE ONE GROUP OF BIRDS THAT EASED HIS LIVING
WEDDED BLISSFUL WITHOUT ISSUE WHILE THOSE TRAPPED VOICES
METICULOUSLY CAGED IN MULTISTORIED CONSTRUCTS ABOVE VAST
FLOORS BENEATH LOW BEAMS EXULTED AS HUMAN SINGERS CAN ONLY
DREAM THIS COUPLE EVEN BEING VERY CLOSE AND HIS WIFE SOME
YEARS THE YOUNGER VERY CULTIVATED TOO AND A PARTICULARLY
GIFTED MUSICIAN WHICH TASTES SHE HAS INSTILLED IN HIM AS
BARLEY ENGENDERS BARLEY THE LION A LION AND GOLD GOLD VIZ
TWO VOICE BOXES ALLOWING HIM FREQUENTLY TO PERFORM
DEMANDING SCORES WITH HER IN CONSEQUENCE OF WHICH SUCH A
CREATURE CAN DO TWO DIFFERENT THINGS AT ONCE WITH ITS THROAT
EVEN SING A DUET WITH ITSELF AND WHETHER ALONE OR WITH HER
HE IS WELL UP IN BOOKS MISSES NOTHING AT ALL AND IT S OBVIOUS
IN TALKING WITH HIM HOW THOSE LITTLE BIRDS PRODUCE SUCH BIG
BEAUTIFUL SONGS WHEN THROUGHOUT THE AUTUMN MONTHS THE
WHISPER OF THE WIND IN THE CORNFIELD IS FOREVER AUDIBLE AS
THE GRAIN WHICH IS SOWN IN CORRUPTION BUT IS RAISED TO
INCORRUPTION POURS INTO THE GIANT HOPPERS AND IS EXALTED FOR
HE IS READ AND SENSIBLE WHAT INSTRUMENT CAN CRAFT SUCH MUSIC
AT THE RATE OF SEVERAL THOUSAND BUSHELS AN HOUR AND THIS C
HAS HAD EXCELLENT VISION ALWAYS SO THAT AGAINST THOSE MANY
WHO WOULD ENTICE FRAIL BIRDS TO SING WITH FIBREOPTIC SCOPES
DOWN THEIR SKINNY THROTTLES DURING HIS YEARS IN TEXTILES
PURSUIT TURNED HABIT AS C MERELY DEMURRED YOU DO NOT RULE
ME CLOUDS OF BLOOD WILL COME TO YOU THEN STRAINED HIS
PEEPERS CONJURING NEW DESIGNS TO PLOT DOWN ON MM^2 GRAPH
PAPER OR IN NUMBERING THE THREADS IN A FABRIC IN WHICH THE
SHAPE OF THE MASS OF DAUGHTER CELLS THAT EMERGES IS USUALLY A
BALL ALTHOUGH IN BIRDS SOMETIMES A SHEET AND HE HAD NEVER
SUFFERED THE LEAST MIGRAINE THOUGH WITH UPPER VOCAL TRACT
IMMOBILISED OR THE LEAST CEREBRAL PROBLEMS DISPASSIONATE
EVEN IN AN EXPERIMENTAL AND WHOLLY ARTIFICIAL ATMOSPHERE
BEFORE THAT FALL WHEN THEY PLOUGHED HIM DOWN AS MME C

RELATED AND THE TASK OF TRANSLATION BEGAN 2 ONE DAY AS SHE
WASHED FROM A SILVER VESSEL MOUNTED WITH FOUR GOLDEN BIRDS
WHILE ATTENTIVE TO THEIR BREATHING AND THE ACTION OF THE
THROAT ON SONG HER HUSBAND ABRUPTLY ENDURED SEVERAL SHARP
STROKES OF SENSELESSNESS IN HIS RIGHT LEG AS THE HUMID SEED
BEGAN TO SWEAT FURTHER INTO DORMANCY AND IN THE SUCCEEDING
DAYS FELT SEVERAL MORE SUCH BROADCAST ON WIDE PERFORATED
FLOORS YET COULD THE WHILE RAMBLE ABROAD UNTIL GRADUALLY
HIS RIGHT ARM AND LEG GREW WEAK AND HE CAME TO KNOW THAT
HE COULD READ NOT A WORD THOUGH HIS SCRIPT AND SPEECH
STAYED UP TO SCRATCH AND HE COULD TELL AS CLEARLY AS EVER FOLK
AND THINGS ARRAYED SO THEN SUSPECTING THAT THE PROBLEM LAY
WITH HIS EYES HE VISITED MY COLLEAGUE TO INTERROGATE THE
THRUSH HOW IT CAN SING SO LOUD AND HE IN TURN REFERRED TO ME
THIS SUBJECT IN WHOM WAS MANIFEST A MARKED AGRAPHIA ALONG
WITH FADED AND COLORLESS VISION ON THE RIGHT ALTHOUGH TO
UNDERSTAND YOU HAVE ONLY TO HUNT DOWN THE SYRINX THAT
VOCAL ORGAN WHICH CONCEALS ITSELF BY CHANNELS DEEP BELOW
THE NECK SO THAT WHEN READING AN EYE CHART C CAN IDENTIFY NO
LETTER THOUGH HE CLAIMS PERFECTLY TO DISCERN THE SYRINX
LYING LOW WITHIN THE BODY AND INSTINCTIVELY HE SKETCHES THE
SHAPES OF THE LETTERS WITH HIS HAND BUT CAN T UTTER EVEN ONE
OF THEIR NAMES FOR BIRDS DON T BREATHE LIKE YOU AND I HAVING
INSTEAD AIR SACS TO PUMP AIR THROUGH THE LUNGS WHERE A
SMOKELESS HEAT RISES FROM BELOW DRIVING THE DRENCHED AIR UP
AND THOUGH MUCH MOVED HE CAN SCARCELY EVEN RECOPY THE
LETTERS LINE BY LINE AS IF PLOTTING A TECHNICAL DRAWING
SCRUTINIZING EACH STROKE TO REASSURE HIMSELF HIS DRAWING IS
EXACT AND BONEDRY AFTER ONE CIRCADIAN CYCLE IT GOES IN STORE
ENCLOSED BY ONE OF THESE SACS AS IT MUST DREAM UNDISTURBED
FOR AT LEAST THREE WEEKS BEFORE TRANSLATION RECOMMENCE BUT
STILL THE NAMES OF LETTERS REMAIN LOST TO HIM AS HE SAYS THE A
IS AN EASEL Z IS A SERPENT AND P A BUCKLE THOUGH THIS WILL NOT
APPEAR QUITE SO FARFETCHED GIVEN HOW CERTAIN INARTICULATE
SOUNDS DO RESEMBLE PARTICULAR LETTERS AS THE TREMBLING OF
WATER IS LIKE THE LETTER L THE QUENCHING OF HOT THINGS THE
LETTER Z THE JIRKING OF A SWITCH THE LETTER Q &C BY AN EXACT
OBSERVATION OF WHICH PARTICULARS IT MAY BE POSSIBLE TO MAKE A
STATUE SPEAK SOME WORDS AND YET THIS FRAUGHT INCAPACITY
FRIGHTENS THE PATIENT C BOUND SO NARROW IN A TANGLE OF
MUSCLE NEAR THE HEART THE NUT SHAPED SYRINX PITEOUSLY TO
CHAUNGE HIR SHAPE THE WATER NYMPHES BESOUGHT AND THINKS
HE HAS GONE MAD SINCE WELL HE KNOWS THE SIGNS THAT HE CAN T

NAME ARE LETTERS AND WHILE STUMBLING CAN TELL NUMERAL FROM
LETTER REMAINS UNABLE TO READ HIS OWN COPIES OF THOSE LETTERS
THEY BEING QUITE IRREGULAR WITH Z REMADE INTO A 7 OR A 1 AND
THE STROKES FEEBLE OR OUT OF PLACE HOW QUICK DO EVIL
COMMUNICATIONS CORRUPT GOOD MANNERS 3 CONSIDER THEN THAT
WHEREAS IN DUCKS CHICKENS PARROTS AND OTHER SUCH DOMESTIC
PRIMITIVES THE SYRINX LODGES IN THE WINDPIPE JUST ABOVE THAT
BRANCHING WHICH SERVES THE LUNGS WHERE IT DRINKS DEEP UNTIL
WATERLOGGED HE HAS NO DIFFICULTIES REMEMBERING IN SUCH A
COMPANY AND THOUGH FEARFUL OF EXPRESSING HIMSELF
NONETHELESS SPEAKS FLUENTLY AND WITHOUT ERROR CRYING OUT AT
TIMES ATTEND GOOD NEWS NEWS FROM THE LODGING THROUGHWAY
FOR SHIPS MEN GLEAMING ACCOUTRED BOASTING OF HURT GREAT
DOWNFALL FAIR FEMALE ON WHOM THE RED THREADWORK OF
SLAUGHTER HAS SETTLED ATTENDING TO SONGBIRDS SUCH AS
WARBLERS LARKS AND SPARROWS YOU WILL SEE A DOUBLE STRUCTURE
THAT SITS A LITTLE LOWER STILL ONE PART WITHIN EACH DIVISION
AND IF THEN SHOWN ANY OBJECTS HE WILL NAME THEM STRAIGHT
OFF INCLUDING ALL THOSE MACHINE COMPONENTS ILLUSTRATED IN A
TECHNICAL INDUSTRIAL HANDBOOK AND NOT ONCE DOES HE
MANIFEST ANY PROBLEM WITH RECALL IMMEDIATELY NAMING AND
IDENTIFYING THE PURPOSE OF ALL THE OBJECTS PICTURED IN THE
MANUAL UNTIL THEY SPROUT AND RAMIFY ABOUT HIM SWEETLY
ENACTING THEIR EXOTIC AND ACCELERATED SPRING BUT THESE
UNTIMELY GERMINATIONS POSED NO PROBLEM FOR ONE AVIAN
ANATOMIST WHO SHEW D A WAY OF MAKING MUSICAL AND OTHER
SOUNDS BY THE STRIKING OF THE TEETH OF SEVERAL BRASS WHEELS
PROPORTIONALLY CUT AS TO THEIR NUMBERS AND TURNED VERY FAST
ROUND IN WHICH IT IS OBSERVABLE THAT THE EQUAL OR PROPORTIONAL
STROAKS OF THE TEETH I E 2 TO 1 4 TO 3 &C MAKE THE MUSICAL
NOTES BUT THE UNEQUAL STROAKS MORE ANSWER THE SOUND OF THE
VOICE AS IT SPEAKS OUT ATTEND GOOD NEWS OUR HORSES EXHAUSTED
WE RIDE AND WE RIDE ON UNCANNY STEEDS THOUGH ALIVE WE ARE
DEAD GREAT SEVERING OF LIVES LONG GORGING OF RAVENS BANQUET
FOR CROWS RATTLE OF SLAUGHTER WHISTLE OF EDGES SHIELDS
SHATTERED IN THE HOURS AFTER SUNSET ATTENDING THE WHILE THE
NIGHT SINGER IN THE UNSTABLE RUSHES BROODS ON A CLUTCH OF
STARS 4 BY THIS TIME THE ACROSPIRE HAS ALMOST BREACHED THE
HUSK AND THE STARCH IS SOFT AND CHALKY AND WHEN YOU CAN
WRITE YOUR NAME ON THE WALL WITH THE EAR IT S READY WHEREFORE
WHEN HE IS SHOWN HIS REGULAR NEWSPAPER C RECOGNIZES IT
CORRECTLY BY THE LAYOUT BUT IS UNABLE TO MAKE OUT ANY OF THE
LETTERS IN THE HEADLINES JUST AS RESEARCHERS HAVE LONG MADE

DO WITH INDIRECT APPROACHES SNIPPING THIS OR THAT MUSCLE
AND WAITING TO ASCERTAIN IT S EFFECT ON THE BIRD S SONG THOUGH
TEXTS ARE SOMETIMES EQUIPPED WITH WORD DIVIDERS WHICH
SIMPLIFIES THINGS BUT IF THESE ARE NOT SUPPLIED THEN THE
READER MUST EDIT HIS TEXT BY STUDYING THE REPETITIONS AND
BREAK THE TEXT UP INTO ITS CONSTITUENT UNITS AS FOR INSTANCE
IF THE PRECEDING PASSAGE WERE RUN TOGETHER STUDY WOULD
SHOW THAT THE SEQUENCE THE FREQUENTLY RECURS AND MUST
THEREFORE BE SOME COMMON WORD AND FURTHERMORE WHEN
SHOWN ANOTHER NEWSPAPER WHOSE FORMAT HE DOES NOT KNOW
AND WHOSE CONSTITUENT WOOD AND RAGS ARE PULPED BEYOND
RECOVERY BY THE EYE C AFTER 5 MINUTES OF THOUGHT MISIDENTIFIES
IT THOUGH AFTER A SPELLING LESSON OF 15 MINUTES HE IS FINALLY
ABLE TO READ THE TITLE BUT IN ORDER TO RECALL THE LETTERS HE
HAD SURGICALLY TO IMPLANT TINY DEVICES TO MEASURE AIRFLOW IN
THE BRANCHED PASSAGES OF TWO SPECIES OF SONGBIRDS NAMELY THE
GREY CATBIRD AND THE BROWN THRASHER SO THAT WHEN THEY
RESUMED THEIR SONG A FEW DAYS LATER THEY SANG OUT CLEAR THE
INTIMATE INJUNCTION HE WILL NOT KILL BIRDS AND C COULD TELL
EXACTLY WHICH NOTES CAME FROM EACH OF THEIR TWO VOICES AND
DRAW THEIR FORM WITH A GESTURE OF THE HAND WHILE NOT
LOOKING AT THE NEWSPAPER BUT THE FURNACE RAGED AGAIN HALTING
ALL DEVELOPMENT AND THESE INTIMATIONS HE STORED AWAY FOR A
TIME 5 WHILE UNABLE TO READ THE PATIENT DOES COPY HIS NAME
CORRECTLY AND WRITES FLUENTLY AND WITHOUT MISTAKE WHATEVER
MATERIAL IS DICTATED TO HIM SINCE THE PAIRED SYRINX PROVIDES A
VARIED TOOL BOX FOR CONSTRUCTING COMPLEX SONGS BUT SHOULD
HE BE INTERRUPTED IN THE MIDDLE OF A PHRASE DURING DICTATION
HE IS QUITE SHATTERED AND CAN T RESTART THOUGH THE THRASHER
SING A TRUE DUET IN WHICH BOTH STONES GRIND AT THE SAME TIME
TO ADD HARMONIC COMPLEXITY AND IF HE MAKES A MISTAKE HE CAN
T FIND IT AND WHILE HE USED TO WRITE FAST AND FINE NOW HIS
LETTERS GROW COARSE AND HESITANT FOR AS HE SAYS HE NO LONGER
HAS CONTROL OF HIS EYES SO THAT ONE SIDE MIGHT FAVOUR A RISING
NOTE THE OTHER A FALLING SAY SO THAT IN FACT RATHER THAN HELP
HIM LOOKING WHILE HE WRITES DISTURBS HIM TO THE POINT THAT
HE PREFERS TO KEEP HIS EYES CLENCHED AND WAIT WHILE SUCH AS
THE BROWN COWBIRD SING RAPID FIRE BURSTS IN WHICH THE TWO
SIDES ALTERNATE NOTES IN A STRATEGY THAT MAY ALLOW EACH TO
GRIND EXCEEDING SMALL WITHOUT RAGGED TRANSITIONS THUS I AM
KING OF YOUR FATHER S BIRD TROOP AND YOU MUST NEVER CAST AT
BIRDS FOR THROUGH KINSHIP EVERY BIRD HERE IS NATURAL TO YOU
UNTIL NOW I DID NOT KNOW THIS HE SAYS LOOKING AS HE WRITES

MIXES HIM UP SO WHEN HIS DISORDER FIRST SET IN AND HE TRIED TO WRITE HE LAID THE LETTERS DOWN ONE ON TOP OF THE OTHER AND THUS WHEN HE WROTE HIS FIRST NAME OSCAR HE PUT THE C ON TOP OF THE S NOW HE WRITES FROM MEMORY WHATEVER HE DESIRES WHETHER IT BE HIS OWN SPONTANEOUS WRITING OR AT ANOTHER S DICTATION HE CAN NEVER REREAD WHAT HE HAS WRITTEN EVEN ISOLATED LETTERS DO NOT MAKE SENSE TO HIM HE CAN ONLY RECOGNIZE THEM AFTER A MOMENT S HESITATION AND THEN ONLY BY TRACING THE OUTLINES OF THE LETTER WITH HIS HAND 6 WHEREAS IN MANY BIRDS THE TWO SIDES ACT LIKE THE TUNS AND KIEVES OF A SOUND SYSTEM WITH THE LEFT SIDE SPECIALISING IN LOWER NOTES AND THE RIGHT IN HIGHER WORKING TOGETHER TO PRODUCE SAY THREE REDS MUST NOT PRECEDE YOU WHERE RED DWELLS IT IS THEREFORE THE SENSE OF MUSCULAR MOVEMENT THAT GIVES RISE TO THE LETTER NAME AS THE CARDINAL THAT VIRTUOSO SWEEPS SMOOTHLY UPWARD FROM ABOUT I KHZ TO 7 KHZ LIKE THE FIRST ELEMENT IN A WOLF WHISTLE IN FACT HE CAN EASILY RECOGNIZE LETTERS AND GIVE THEIR NAMES WITH HIS EYES CLOSED BY MOVING HIS HAND THROUGH THE SCALDING WATER FOLLOWING THE OUTLINES OF THE LETTERS NOTING THAT AT ABOUT 3.5 KHZ THE SOUND SWITCHES SEAMLESSLY FROM LEFT TO RIGHT QUITE UNLIKE SPEAKERS C CAN DO SIMPLE ADDITION HOWEVER RECOGNIZING WITH RELATIVE EASE THE CRY OF OSSAR OSSAR THE HOUND BUT IS VERY SLOW READING EACH CHARGE POORLY SINCE HE CAN T RECOGNIZE THE VALUE OF SEVERAL NUMBERS AT ONCE AND THOUGH ONE CAN T SEE OBVIOUS DIFFERENCES IN THIS MISHMASH THAT DOESN T MEAN THEY AREN T THERE FOR WHEN SHOWN THE NUMBER I I 2 HE SAYS IT IS A I A I AND A 2 AND ONLY WHEN HE WRITES THE NUMBER CAN HE SAY ONE HUNDRED AND TWELVE ONLY SUPERFICIALLY IS HIS VOICE MONOTONOUS AND COMPOSED OF A SINGLE VOWEL AAA IN TRUTH IT STATES THE THOROUGH AND IMMENSE WEALTH OF THAT BODY BUT MUCH OF THE SPECIALISATION COULD BE ACCOUNTED FOR BY DIFFERENCES IN MUSCULAR FORCE APPLIED TO THE TWO SIDES SO PERHAPS IT IS A QUESTION REALLY OF GRANULARITY OF SCALE COLD WIND ACROSS A DANGEROUS EDGE NIGHT FOR DESTROYING A KING 7 AND C EMPLOYS HIS DAYS TAKING LONG WALKS WITH HIS WIFE AND COMPLAINS OF NO DIFFICULTY WALKING AND EVERY DAY HE DOES HIS ERRANDS ON FOOT ALONG A LONG FAMILIAR ROUTE FULLY AWARE OF WHAT S HAPPENING AROUND HIM HE STOPS AT THE WOODEN BACKS EXAMINES PAINTINGS IN GALLERY WINDOWS AND ONLY THOSE POSTERS AND SIGNS IN SHOPS SHOWING TOGETHER A BIRD A MOUSE A FROG AND FIVE ARROWS REMAIN SENSELESS COLLECTIONS OF SIGNS OFTEN EXASPERATING HIM FOR THOUGH AFFLICTED FOR FOUR YEARS HE HAS

NEVER ACCEPTED THAT HE CANNOT READ THOUGH CAPABLE OF
WRITING BEING WELL AWARE THAT CANARIES USE THEIR DOUBLE
SYRINX YET OTHERWISE THEY SING THROUGH THE LEFT AND INHALE
THROUGH THE RIGHT SAYING FOR INSTANCE YOU ARE GOING AWAY
YOU LOVE A FOREIGN WOMAN WHO BARS MY WAY TO YOU YOU WILL
HAVE CHILDREN WHO WILL BRING YOU JOY BUT I AM SAD AND THINK
ONLY OF YOU EVEN IF ANOTHER MAN SHOULD COME ALONG AND LOVE
ME AFTER THEIR WALKS M AND MME C PLAY MUSIC TOGETHER UNTIL
DINNER OR MME C READS TO HER HUSBAND BIOGRAPHIES OF
MUSICIANS NOVELS OR THE LATEST NEWS AS FOR EXAMPLE OUR
ENEMIES WILL SURRENDER TO US THEMSELVES THEIR LAND AND SEAS
SINCE A MOUSE IS BRED IN EARTH AND SUBSISTS ON THE FOOD OF MAN
AND A FROG LIVES IN THE WATER AND A BIRD IS VERY LIKE A HORSE
AND THE ARROWS ARE ALL THEIR STRENGTH AND SUCH A STRATEGY IS
POSSIBLE BECAUSE THE LUNGS CONNECT SO THAT A ONE SIDED
INHALATION CAN FILL BOTH LUNGS WHICH DIVISION OF LABOUR IT IS
RECKONED MAY HELP THEM DASH OFF LONG RUNS OF AS MANY AS 30
SHORT   SOUND   SEGMENTS   PER   SECOND   YET   TO   AVOID
SELFSTRANGULATION SOME SINGING CANARIES HAVE BEEN OBSERVED
TO SNEAK A QUICK BREATH AFTER EVERY SYLLABLE SAYING UNLESS YE
BECOME BIRDS AND TAKE TO THE AIR OR MICE AND BURROW INTO THE
EARTH OR FROGS AND SEEK WATER YE SHALL FALL TO THESE SHAFTS
AND FOR EVENING RECREATION THEY AGAIN PLAY MUSIC AND THEN
SOME HANDS OF CARDS FOR HE IS INDEED AN EXCELLENT PLAYER
PLOTTING HIS STROKES WELL IN ADVANCE AND IS IN THE HABIT OF
WINNING SINCE SPEED IT SEEMS MAY BE THE CRUX AS FEMALE CANARIES
PREFER MALES WITH FASTER SONGS AND THE MALES OF OTHER SPECIES
MAY FEEL SIMILAR PRESSURE AS SWEETNESS TRANSLATES TO STRENGTH
ONE MIGHT MAKE UP A TONGUE PALATE TEETH SOME LIPS A NOSE &
SOME SPRINGS WITH MATERIAL & FIGURE LIKE THOSE OF THE VERY
MOUTH AND IMITATE THE ACTION OF THESE ITEMS FOR THE
GENERATION OF WORDS AND THEN ARRANGE THESE ARTIFICIAL
ORGANS IN SOME CONSTRUCT FIXING IT UP TO UTTER NOT ONLY THE
MOST PASSIONATE AIRS BUT ALSO THE MOST EXQUISITE VERSE WASHES
OVER THE EASTERN HORIZON 8 SO AGAIN AND AGAIN C TRIES TO GET
CERTAIN SPARROWS TO SING FASTER BY RECORDING WILD SONGS AND
THEN HEATING THESE RETORTS OVER A FURNACE UNTIL SUBLIMATION
EXPEL ALL NATURAL BREATHS FROM THE HEART OF THE RUN BETWEEN
SYLLABLES WITH THE ROAR AS OF A GREAT WIND AND FROM TIME TO
TIME HE GROWS AGITATED AND CANNOT ABIDE BUT PACES TO AND FRO
USING THESE BREATHLESS SONGS LIKE THE AVIAN EQUIVALENT OF FINE
PRINT IN RADIO ADVERTS TO CHARGE YOUNG SPARROWS THAT HAVE
NEVER HEARD A NORMAL SONG AND TWICE HE FEINTS STRANGLING

HIS WIFE AND THEN HIMSELF AFTERWARDS OBSERVING THAT THE
BIRDS DO THEIR BEST TO COPY BUT CAN T KEEP UP FOR MORE THAN A
FEW SYLLABLES BEFORE STOPPING AS IF TO CATCH THEIR BREATH
UNTIL ONE DAY HE OVERHEARS SOMEONE SAYING THAT THE SUREST
WAY TO A STILL HEAD IS TO JUMP OFF THE TOP OF A NOTABLE
MONUMENT WHERE IT IS HEARD AGAIN THE CRY OF OSSAR OSSAR THE
HOUND WHICH IDEA BECOMES FIXED IN HIM AND HE SPEAKS OF IT
WHEN EXCITED SO IT BECOMES EVIDENT THAT EVEN A MINOR INCREASE
IN TRILL RATE GIVES RISE TO DISTURBANCE SUGGESTING THAT SONGS
IN THE WILD ARE AT THE EDGE WHEREUPON ONE DAY HE GOES ALONE
TO THIS MONUMENT AND ASKS THE GUARD PERMISSION TO VISIT THE
INTERIOR BUT THE GUARD REFUSES TO LET HIM ENTER SAYING THAT
VISITS ARE NO LONGER PERMITTED SINCE TWO PEOPLE COMMITTED
SUICIDE IN THE SAME WEEK BY JUMPING OFF THE TOP OF THE
MONUMENT AH THE WORM HE SAYS HAS BROUGHT THEIR SPIRITS LOW
AND HE WONDERED AGAIN AT THE BIRDSONG DECLARATIONS OF WAR
A PEOPLE DESTROYED THE RUIN OF A LODGING MEN WOUNDED
DESPONDENT A TERRIBLE WIND WITH LOSS OF DEFENCES
UNSUSTAINABLE PAIN MEANINGS FORGOTTEN ALIEN HEIRS HARVESTS
UNCUT A SHOUTING A SCREAM BUT WHETHER THE BIRDS WHISTLE
LIKE A KETTLE BY FORCING AIR THROUGH A STRAIT VENT IN THE
SYRINX OR BUZZ LIKE A KAZOO RATTLING THE FLIMSY DRUM BESIDE
EACH OUTLET THE FIERCE UPSHOT MAKES THE SPIRIT SAFE 9
FOLLOWING THIS PERIOD OF AGITATION HIS HAND GROWS IRREGULAR
AND MUST BE COOPED AND C WILL NO LONGER INTERROGATE LIVING
BIRDS BUT RATHER THE EXCISED SYRINX OF A PRECIOUS FINCH WHICH
NORMAL MUSCLE TONE HAS DESERTED AND HIS ORIENTATION REMAINS
EXACT ALTHOUGH IN SPITE OF PATIENT LABOUR HE CAN T ACCESS THE
KNOWLEDGE OF THE LIVING BOOK REVEALED TO THE EMANATIONS AS
LETTERS WHICH ARE NOT VOWELS NOR ARE THEY CONSONANTS THAT
ONE MIGHT MISREAD FOOLISHLY BUT ARE RATHER THE LETTERS OF
THE TRUTH WHICH THEY ALONE SPEAK WHO KNOW THEM NOR CAN
HE AGAIN DECIPHER A TABLATURE BUT THAT SYRINX QUELLED IN
BOND BETRAYS THE ACTION OF THE HUMAN APPARATUS WHILE WHO
KNOW NOT THAT WHEREOF THEY SPEAK ATTEMPT TO MIMIC VOICE
WITH RIGS AND INSTRUMENTS YET HE CAN MASTER UNFAMILIAR MUSIC
EVEN REHEARSE THE INTACT BODY OF TWO NEW WORKS AS HIS WIFE
PLAYS FOR HIM SINGS THEM WITH HIM FEEDING HIM THE KEEPSAKE
WORDS SO THAT AFTER A LITTLE PRACTICE HE CAN UNDERTAKE ONE IN
ITS ENTIRETY WITHOUT HER SUPPLYING THE SLIGHTEST CLUE FOR
EVEN A SINGLE SYLLABLE WHEREUPON TO THEIR SURPRISE THEY
OBSERVE THE SYRINX OPERATE NOT LIKE A KAZOO OR WHISTLE BUT
RESEMBLING THE HUMAN VOICE AS IN SONG TAUT MUSCLES DRAW

THOSE TWO HEAVY FOLDS OF TISSUE THE INTERNAL AND EXTERNAL
LABIA INTO THE VAULT WHERE OUTRUSHING AIR SETS THEM VIBRATING
JUST LIKE HUMAN VOCAL CORDS WHEN EACH SLIGHT UTTERANCE IS A
COHERENT THOUGHT COMPACT AS A BOOK AND HE RETAINS A PERFECT
NOTION OF MUSICAL RHYTHM AS THIS QUASI KAZOO DOESN T AFFECT
SOUND MUCH AT ALL SINCE WHEN HE DESTROYS IT SURGICALLY PITCH
AND VOLUME ALTER ONLY IMPERCEPTIBLY 10 MIDWINTER SEVERAL
YEARS LATER DURING A HAND OF CARDS C DECLARES THAT THE
CHILDREN OF THE FATHER ARE HIS FRAGRANCE AND IS AFFLICTED
WITH PINS AND NEEDLES IN THE RIGHT LEG AND ARM AND A
GATHERING AND INSUFFERABLE THIRST WHICH PERSISTS AS THE
DELICATE ETHERS GATHER AND RESOLVE AND WHILE SOME COLLEAGUES
FOUND AN INTRIGUING HINT THAT THE SYRINX MAY RUN ON
AUTOPILOT FOR A SPELL ONE WENT IN SEARCH OF LIVING WATER FOR
HIS KING SINCE THE SONG OF THAT PRECIOUS FINCH SOMETIMES
CHANGES ABRUPTLY FROM A PURE TONE TO A NOISY BUZZ AND BACK
AGAIN AS HE LOVES HIS FRAGRANCE AND MANIFESTS IT IN EVERY PLACE
AND IF IT MIXES WITH MATTER HE GIVES HIS FRAGRANCE TO THE
LIGHT AND IN HIS REPOSE HE CAUSES IT TO SURPASS EVERY FORM AND
SOUND AS HIS DETERIORATION PROCEEDS UTTERING ONE WORD IN
PLACE OF ANOTHER OR GARBLING SOUNDS AS IT IS A CHILD WHO IS
AGED IT IS GRIEVOUS HIS SHORTNESS OF LIFE THOUGH HE CAN MIMIC
EXTREMELY WELL WHICH IS A HALLMARK OF A SYSTEM ON THE EDGE
OF CHAOS AND AN EXCISED SYRINX EXHIBITS THE SAME SUDDEN
SWITCHES WHEN AIR IS FORCED THROUGH IT AT GRADUALLY
INCREASING SPEEDS SO HE CAN MAKE HIS WIFE UNDERSTAND WHAT
HE WANTS THROUGH GESTURES AND SIGNS OF AFFIRMATION OR
NEGATION BUT HIS WIFE GIVES HIM A PENCIL AND NOTICES WITH
DREAD THAT HE CAN NO LONGER WRITE TRACING ON THE PAPER
STROKES AND LINES WITHOUT ANY APPARENT SENSE HA HA HA HA HA
THIRST WHICH SUGGESTS THAT SIMPLE CHANGES IN AIRFLOW RATHER
THAN ELABORATE ORCHESTRATION BY THE BRAIN MAY ACCOUNT FOR
SOME OF THE RICHNESS OF THE FINCH S SONG AND INDEED MUCH OF
ITS STRUCTURE IS MADE AT ONCE EXPLICABLE BY REGARDING THE
SYRINX AS MACHINE RATHER THAN AS AGENT AND AS HE SIGHED WITH
HIS BREATH THE REEDES HE SOFTLY SHOOKE TREMBLING FAR OUT
UNDER THE CITY S COURTS AND THOROUGHFARES CHURCHES
TERRACES AND MARKETS FOR IF THE SYRINX IS THE MOUTHPIECE OF A
TRUMPET THEN A BIRD S THROAT AND MOUTH PLAY THE PARTS OF THE
TUBING VALVES AND BELL AND RESONANCES HERE MODIFY ENORMOUSLY
THE CRY OF OSSAR OSSAR THE HOUND AS IT PASSES THROUGH AND
YOU MAY EASILY HEAR THIS EFFECT IN HUMANS WHERE THE THROAT
MOUTH AND LIPS FORM ALL THE VARIOUS VOWEL AND CONSONANT

SOUNDS OF SPEECH AS WELL AS ISSUING THOSE MANIFOLD DIFFERENCES
IN TIMBRE THAT MAKE AN ABUNDANCE OF SPECTRES AND CONSTITUTE
THE ANGELS SHARE FOR IT IS NOT THE EARS THAT SMELL THE
FRAGRANCE BUT THE BREATH THAT CAN SENSE SMELL AND ATTRACTS
THE FRAGRANCE TO ITSELF AND IS OVERWHELMED AS THE
CHARACTERISTIC FLAVOUR AND AROMA AND BOUQUET ARE BORN AND
NURTURED TO FULL RICHNESS AND HE SHELTERS IT AND HOLDS IT
WHERE IT CAME FROM FROM THAT FIRST FRAGRANCE WHICH IS NOW
GROWN COLD I I C S INTELLIGENCE REMAINS INTACT HE UNDERSTANDS
ALL QUESTIONS PUT TO HIM AND IS ATTENTIVE TO ALL THAT GOES ON
AROUND HIM HIS MIMIC IS EXTREMELY EXPRESSIVE AND HIS PANTOMIME
VERY ARRESTING BUT WHO TALKS HAVING INSPIRED THE SIMPLEST OF
NOBLE ELEMENTS SHRILLS AS THAT LIGHT MEDIUM CONDUCTS SOUNDS
FASTER AND STRESSES RESONANCES IN THE VOCAL TRACT AT SOARING
PITCHES THOUGH THE VIBRATION OF THE VOCAL CORDS CHANGE
LITTLE SO THE UPPER VOCAL TRACT ACTS AS A FILTER PRODUCING
PUREST TONES BY AMPLIFYING CERTAIN UTTERANCES FROM THE SYRINX
WHICH MADE A STILL AND MOURNING NOYSE BUT AS MANY SONGS
LEAP ABOUT FROM FLAVOUR TO FLAVOUR BIRDS MUST CONSTANTLY
ADJUST THE FILTER TO ADMIT JUST THE RIGHT TONES WHICH FILMED
SPARROWS CORROBORATE AS SINGING THEY MAY BE SEEN TO OPEN
THEIR BEAKS WIDER FOR HIGH NOTES THUS ABBREVIATING THEIR
VOCAL TRACT AND MAKING IT RESONATE AT A HIGHER FREQUENCY
THOUGH ALL BE ULTIMATELY BROUGHT TO UNISON AND AT THAT
JUNCTURE C REMEMBERING THAT HIS NIECE CAME FOR LUNCH EVERY
SATURDAY IN ORDER TO TELL HIS WIFE THAT HE DID NOT WANT THE
NIECE TO COME ON SATURDAY DID AS FOLLOWS FIRST GOT UP WENT TO
THE DINING ROOM AND SET THE TABLE FOR THE THREE OF THEM AS
USUAL HIS NIECE HIS WIFE AND SELF HIS WIFE UNDERSTOOD YOU
WANT TO TALK ABOUT YOUR NIECE SIGN OF APPROVAL SHE MUST BE
WRITTEN TO LIVELY SIGNS OF APPROVAL TELL HER THAT YOU ARE SICK
ENERGETIC SIGN OF DISAPPROVAL WRITE AND TELL HER NOT TO COME
LIVELY SIGNS OF APPROVAL AND OF SATISFACTION ON THE PART OF THE
PATIENT AT WHOSE FEET FALLS STRAIGHT A NIGHTINGALE OF STONE
AND IS IT NOT SOMETHING IN A PSYCHIC FORM RESEMBLING COLD
WATER WHICH HAS FROZEN OVER EARTH THAT IS NOT SOLID OF WHICH
THOSE WHO SEE IT THINK IT IS EARTH AND AFTERWARDS IT DISSOLVES
AGAIN AND SAVAGE IS THE ANSWER LET HER IN I 2 IN SEEDS ARE GERMS
THAT HAPPENING IN WATER BECOME FILAMENTS OR BETWEEN WATER
AND EARTH ARE SLIME OR WHEN THEY FIGURE IN EXALTED SITES MARK
A PROFOUND MUTABILITY AND SO IN AN EXPERIMENT YET TO BE
PUBLISHED RESEARCHERS IMMOBILISE THE KING AND STRIKE OFF HIS
HEAD ATTEMPTING THEREBY TO REPLICATE AN EARLIER RESULT IN

WHICH THEY HELD SPARROWS BEAKS AT A FIXED GAPE BY CLAMPING
THEM FOR BRIEF PERIODS TO A BITE BLOCK AND AFTER A FEW DAYS
TRAINED THEM TO SING WITH THEIR BEAKS CLAMPED SO THE
MUTABILITY IS RECOVERED FROM FINE TILTH AS CROW S FOOT ITS
ROOTS LARVAE ITS LEAVES BUTTERFLIES AND THIS THE BODY THOUGH
SURE ENOUGH THOSE BIRDS DID SING MORE LOFTY AND MORE SHRILL
WHEN HE POURED DRINK STRAIGHT INTO THE PARCHED GULLET AND
CRIED ALOUD WHO BRINGS DRINK TO A KING DOES WELL WITH
OVERTONES THE STRAUNGENESSE OF THE WHICH AND SWEETNESS OF
THE FEEBLE SOUNDE FOUND ON THE MORNING OF JANUARY 16TH
1892 THE CONSUMED C QUITE STILL QUITE GONE QUITE PATIENT YET
THE BUTTERFLIES EVOLVE TO FRASS AND INFESTATION UNDERNEATH
THE FIRE AND SO LIKE EXUVIAE THAT THEY ARE CALLED HOUSE
CRICKETS WHICH AFTER A THOUSAND DAYS TRANSLATE TO BIRDS
KNOWN AS DRIED SURPLUS BONES AND THE SPITTLE OF THE DRIED
SURPLUS BONES TURNS TO A FINE SPARGE WHERE IS THE PALATE
SITUATE AND THAT MIST FALLS AS MATRIX OF BITTERNESS AS AUTOPSY
REVEALED A RECENT LESION AND AN OLD ALONG WITH EVIDENCE OF
THE DESTRUCTION OF CERTAIN FIBRE TRACTS DURING THAT FOREGOING
PERIOD IN WHICH HIS FACULTIES WERE MASHED AND WASHED AND
RECTIFIED AND THE DRAFF DID FATTEN STALLED AND STABLE BEASTS
BUT THIS BROUGHT ON A FURTHER VISITATION WHEREFORE THOSE
FRAGRANCES THAT ARE COLD ARE FROM THESE BREAKDOWNS WHICH
PROVOKED WARMTH TO SUPERVENE AND DO AWAY WITH ALL DIVISION
SO THE COLD SHOULD NOT COME AGAIN THAT THERE SHOULD INSTEAD
BE IDEAL UNISON AND THEY HAVE TAKEN HIS VERY HEART S BLOOD
AND DRANK IT ROUND AND ROUND WHERE YELLOW WHIRLIGIGS
SPRING OUT OF LOW WINES BLIND FLIES ARE BORN FROM THESE
CORRUPTIONS AND WHEN A LIVING STRAND COUPLES WITH A DORMANT
STEM START THINGS WITH NO SENSIBLE NAME RECURRING AS
PANTHERS PANTHERS THEN AS HORSES HORSES MEN WHO WILL
RETURN DISPIRITED TO THAT GENERAL CONCOURSE
OR AT THE FINISH BREATHE BEYOND THE
SONET NOTES STONE TONES ONSET

(For Angela, 2001)

Lightning Source UK Ltd.
Milton Keynes UK
UKOW03f2055250117
292886UK00001B/217/P

9 781848 613522